MIXER & BLENDER COOKING

Edited by
Hilary Walden

CONTENTS

This edition first published 1978 by
Octopus Books Limited
59 Grosvenor Street, London W.1.

ISBN 0 7064 0701 6

Produced and printed in Hong Kong by
Mandarin Publishers Limited
22a Westlands Road, Quarry Bay

Frontispiece: MIDSUMMER MERINGUE *(page 67) (Photograph: Gale's Honey)*

Weights and Measures

All measurements in this book are based on Imperial weights and measures, with American equivalents given in parenthesis.

Measurements in *weight* in the Imperial and American system are the same. Measurements in *volume* are different, and the following table shows the equivalents:

Spoon measurements

Imperial	U.S.
1 tablespoon	1 tablespoon
1½ tablespoons	2 tablespoons
2 tablespoons	3 tablespoons (abbrev: T)

Level spoon measurements are used in all the recipes.

Liquid measurements

1 Imperial pint	20 fluid ounces
1 American pint	16 fluid ounces
1 American cup	8 fluid ounces

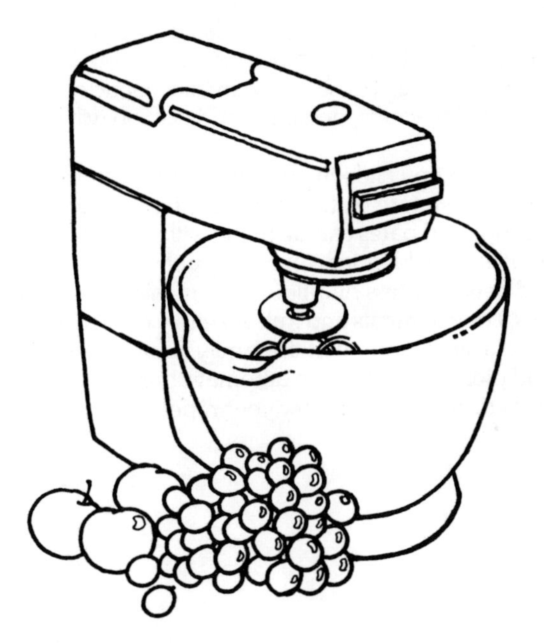

INTRODUCTION

In recent years there has been an increase in the number of labour saving appliances available to the housewife, not the least being in the field of cooking.

Unfortunately, often the full potential of the equipment is not realized and it is only used to a limited extent, spending most of the time hidden away in a cupboard. To avoid 'out of sight, out of mind' keep your mixer and blender on a working surface, if you have enough space in your kitchen.

The aim of this book is to show how mixers and blenders can not only be used for the basic tasks, such as cake and pastry making, but can help in the preparation of all manner of dishes from the everyday to the more complicated 'dinner-party' type where they can really be made to earn their keep. Part of the secret is to get into the habit of using the equipment for chores like chopping vegetables, grating cheese, making breadcrumbs and sauces. Then your mixer and blender can be employed in several stages in the making of one dish.

There are now many types of mixers and blenders available in the shops today. Your choice will largely depend on your personal needs but it is worth considering the advantages that different models offer before buying.

Mixers vary in size from the small hand mixers to the large stand models. Obviously large mixers enable you to prepare larger quantities of food and are useful for batch baking cakes, bread and pastry. Attachments can also be obtained for these models. These include shredders, juice extractors, dough hooks and mincers which increase the versatility of the equipment. If you have a large family this type of mixer should prove to be a real time saver and take a lot of the effort out of cooking.

Hand mixers are ideal for preparing smaller quantities of food. They have the additional advantage that they can be used for beating and mixing in almost any bowl or saucepan. This is particularly useful for preparing sauces, choux pastry and soufflés.

Blenders or liquidizers, as they are sometimes called, also vary in size. It is usually possible to obtain a blender as an attachment for a large mixer but there is also a range of free standing models now available. Those with a smaller capacity can cope with most blending tasks but when making soups, desserts or drinks you will need to work with smaller quantities.

A blender is a real asset in any kitchen. Purées, stuffings, sauces and salad dressings which are time consuming to prepare by hand will only take a few minutes in a blender. Delicious home-made soups and pâtés can be made with the minimum of effort.

If you have a young family a blender can certainly save you money. Canned baby foods are expensive and generally less nutritious than meals prepared in the kitchen. Fresh cooked vegetables, cooked meats and fruit are easily puréed in the blender and it is often convenient to blend a small portion of the family meal for toddlers.

Once the mixer and blender become an automatic part of your cooking, you will be surprised at the time and effort saved and how your repertoire of recipes increases.

TUNA AND OLIVE PIE *(page 51) (Photograph: Olives from Spain)*

MARJORAM

BASIC RECIPES

Shortcrust Pastry (Basic Pie Dough)

8 oz. (2 cups) plain (all-purpose) flour
pinch of salt
2 oz. (¼ cup) butter
2 oz. (¼ cup) lard (shortening)
3 tablespoons (¼ cup) cold water

Sift the flour and salt into the mixer bowl. Roughly chop the butter and lard into the bowl and turn the mixer to a slow speed. Gradually increase the speed until the mixture resembles fine breadcrumbs. Switch off immediately, taking care not to overmix.

Sprinkle the water over the mixture and gently bind together with a knife to form a ball. Chill for 30 minutes before rolling out and using as required.

Makes 8 oz. shortcrust pastry (basic pie dough)

Sweet Flan Pastry

4 oz. (1 cup) plain (all-purpose) flour
2 oz. (¼ cup) butter, roughly chopped
½ oz. (2T) icing (confectioners') sugar
½ teaspoon salt
1 egg yolk
3 teaspoons water
1 teaspoon lemon juice

Place the flour in a bowl. Add the butter and mix on a low speed until the mixture resembles fine breadcrumbs. Add the sugar and salt.

Mix together the egg yolk and water. Add to the dry ingredients together with the lemon juice and mix on a low speed just until all the ingredients are evenly incorporated. Cover and leave in a cool place for 15 minutes before rolling out and using as required.

Makes 4 oz. sweet flan pastry

Choux Pastry

¼ pint (⅔ cup) water
2 oz. (¼ cup) butter or margarine
3 oz. (¾ cup) plain (all-purpose) flour
½ teaspoon salt
2 eggs, lightly beaten

Place the water and fat in a saucepan and gently bring to the boil. Tip in the flour and salt all at once. Using a hand mixer, beat on a high speed until the mixture comes away from the sides of the pan.

Continuing to beat on high speed, add the eggs a little at a time. The mixture should become thick, smooth and glossy.

Choux puffs:
Spoon the choux pastry into a piping bag fitted with a ½ inch plain nozzle. Pipe small rounds of the mixture on to a greased baking tray, spacing well apart. Bake at 425°F, Gas Mark 7 for 15-20 minutes.

Make a slit in the side of each puff to allow the steam to escape. Cool on a wire tray. Fill with whipped cream and dust with icing (confectioners') sugar.

Makes 12-16 puffs

Éclairs:
Place the mixture in a piping bag fitted with a ½ inch plain nozzle. Pipe 3 inch lengths on to a greased baking tray. Bake at 425°F, Gas Mark 7 for 15-20 minutes.

Remove from the oven, slit the éclairs down one side to let the steam escape and cool on a wire tray. When cold, fill with whipped cream and top with coffee or chocolate glacé icing.

Makes 12-16 éclairs

Batters

Pouring Consistency:
4 oz. (1 cup) plain (all-purpose) flour
½ teaspoon salt
1 egg
½ pint (1¼ cups) milk

Coating Consistency:
4 oz. (1 cup) plain (all-purpose) flour
¼ teaspoon salt
1 egg
¼ pint (⅔ cup) milk

Put the flour, salt, egg and a little of the milk in the blender goblet. Turn the speed to medium and gradually pour in the remaining milk, increasing the speed. Blend to a smooth batter.

Uses:
Coating batter: fritters.
Pouring batter: pancakes, Yorkshire pudding, toad-in-the-hole.

Scones

8 oz. (2 cups) self-raising flour
1 teaspoon salt
½ teaspoon cinnamon (optional)
2 oz. (¼ cup) butter or margarine, cut into pieces
2 oz. (¼ cup) castor (superfine) sugar
1 egg, lightly beaten
4 tablespoons (⅓ cup) milk
2 oz. (⅓ cup) currants (optional)
milk for brushing

Sift the flour, salt and cinnamon, if used, into the mixer bowl. Add the fat and sugar. Mix on a slow speed until the fat is broken up. Increase to maximum speed until the fat is evenly distributed. Reduce the speed to minimum. Add the egg and milk, mixing to form a soft pliable dough. Add the currants, if used.

Turn onto a lightly floured surface and knead until smooth. Roll out to ½ inch thickness and cut into rounds with a 2 inch fluted cutter. Place on a greased baking tray and brush the scones with milk.

Bake in a hot oven, 425°F, Gas Mark 7 for 10 minutes. Cool on a wire rack. Split the scones and serve with butter.

Makes 12 scones

Cheese scones:
Omit the sugar, currants and cinnamon. Grate 2 oz. Cheddar cheese in the blender. Add the cheese, ¼ teaspoon black pepper and ½ teaspoon dry mustard to the scone mixture with the egg and milk. Use a plain cutter to shape the scones. Brush with beaten egg instead of milk before baking.

SAVOURY PANCAKES *(page 46) (Photograph: Danish Food Centre)*

Whisked Sponge

3 eggs
3 oz. (⅓ cup) castor (superfine) sugar
3 oz. (¾ cup) plain (all-purpose) flour
½ teaspoon salt
jam, lemon curd or whipped cream for filling
icing (confectioners') sugar for dusting

Place the eggs and sugar in a warmed bowl and beat on a high speed until light, pale in colour and frothy. The beaters should leave an impression when drawn across the top of the mixture. Sift the flour and salt together. Using a metal spoon, fold the flour into the mixture.

Turn into 2 lightly greased and floured 7 inch sandwich tins and bake in a fairly hot oven, 400°F, Gas Mark 6 for 15-20 minutes. Turn onto a wire tray to cool.

Sandwich the layers together with jam, lemon curd or whipped cream. Dust the top of the cake with sifted icing sugar.
Makes one 7 inch sponge

Genoese sponge:
Proceed as above, whisking in 2 oz. (¼ cup) melted unsalted butter before adding the flour.

Victoria Sandwich

4 oz. (½ cup) butter or margarine, softened
4 oz. (½ cup) castor (superfine) sugar
2 eggs, lightly beaten
2-3 drops vanilla essence
4 oz. (1 cup) self-raising flour
pinch of salt
4 tablespoons (⅓ cup) jam
icing (confectioners') sugar for dusting

Warm the bowl and the beaters. Place the butter or margarine in the bowl and beat on a high speed for 1 minute. Add the sugar and continue to beat until the mixture is light and fluffy. Add the eggs and vanilla essence a little at a time, beating thoroughly on a high speed after each addition.

Reduce to a minimum speed and add the flour and salt. Switch off immediately the flour is evenly incorporated.

Turn into 2 greased 7 inch sandwich tins and bake in a moderate oven, 350°F, Gas Mark 4 for 25 minutes. Turn onto a wire rack to cool.

When cold, spread one layer with the jam, place the other on top and dust with sieved icing sugar.
Makes one 7 inch sandwich cake

Crème Pâtissière

½ pint (1 ¼ cups) milk
1 vanilla pod (bean) split
3 egg yolks
2 oz. (¼ cup) castor (superfine) sugar
¾ oz. (3T) plain (all-purpose) flour
½ oz. (1T) cornflour (cornstarch)
½ oz. (1T) butter, softened
few drops of vanilla or almond essence

Place the milk and vanilla pod (bean) in a saucepan and bring almost to boiling point. Take off the heat, cover and leave to infuse for 15 minutes.

Whisk the egg yolks and sugar on a high speed until thick and light. Lower the speed to medium and beat in the flour and cornflour. Remove the vanilla pod from the milk and pour onto the egg mixture, beating all the time.

Return to the saucepan and bring to the boil over a medium heat, stirring constantly. Boil for 3 minutes. Allow to cool slightly, then pour into the blender goblet. Add the butter and essence and blend for about 15 seconds.

Pour into a bowl and cover with greased greaseproof or waxed paper to prevent a skin forming and leave until cold.

Makes about ½ pint (1¼ cups)

SOUPS AND SAVOURIES

Chilled Cucumber Soup

8 oz. (2 cups) Gouda cheese, cubed
2 cucumbers, roughly chopped
2 tablespoons (3T) lemon juice
1 tablespoon mixed herbs
1 teaspoon salt
½ teaspoon freshly ground black pepper
½ pint (1 ¼ cups) chicken stock (bouillon)
Garnish:
cucumber slices

Place all the ingredients in the blender goblet. Turn the speed to slow, then increase to maximum until thoroughly blended.

Pour into individual bowls or a large tureen and chill thoroughly. Garnish with cucumber slices just before serving.

Serves 6

Cream of Chestnut Soup

2 lb. chestnuts
1 oz. (2T) butter
1 onion, chopped
2 oz. (¼ cup) streaky (fatty) bacon, derinded and chopped
2 sticks celery, chopped
1 medium potato, peeled and quartered
1½ pints (3¾ cups) chicken stock (bouillon)
¼ pint (⅔ cup) single (light) cream
salt
freshly ground black pepper
Garnish:
1 tablespoon chopped fresh parsley
croûtons

Make a slit in both ends of the chestnuts and place in boiling water for 10 minutes. Skin whilst still hot.

Melt the butter and fry the onion gently for 5 minutes until translucent but not browned. Add the bacon and celery and fry for a further 3 minutes, stirring frequently. Add the chestnuts, potato and stock, bring to the boil and simmer gently for 30 minutes.

Pour into the goblet of a blender and emulsify until smooth. Pour in the cream through the centre cavity and blend again for a few seconds. Return to the pan and heat gently, but do not allow to boil.

Check the seasoning and pour into a warmed tureen or individual soup bowls. Sprinkle with chopped parsley and garnish with fried croûtons.

Serves 4-6

CHILLED CUCUMBER SOUP *(Photograph: Dutch Dairy Bureau)*

Tomato Soup

2 oz. (¼ cup) butter
2 slices streaky (fatty) bacon, derinded and chopped
1 medium onion, roughly chopped
1 stick celery, roughly chopped
1½ lb. tomatoes, roughly chopped
1 pint (2½ cups) chicken stock (bouillon)
1 teaspoon salt
½ teaspoon freshly ground black pepper
½ teaspoon paprika
½ teaspoon castor (superfine) sugar
1 teaspoon chervil
1 teaspoon basil

Garnish:
2 tablespoons (3T) chopped chives
4 tablespoons (⅓ cup) soured cream (optional)

Melt the butter and add the bacon, onion and celery. Fry gently for 2 minutes. Add the tomatoes and cook, stirring for 3 minutes. Pour in the stock, seasonings, sugar and herbs. Cover the saucepan and simmer gently for 20 minutes.

Remove the bacon and pour the soup into the blender goblet. Turn to slow speed then gradually increase to maximum and blend until smooth. Return the soup to the saucepan and reheat. Taste and adjust the seasoning if necessary.

Pour into a tureen or individual bowls. Sprinkle with the chives. If soured cream is used, swirl on the top before sprinkling with the chives.

Serves 4

Vichyssoise

1 oz. (2T) butter
3 medium leeks, chopped
1 onion, chopped
1 stick celery, chopped
3 potatoes, peeled and chopped
1½ pints (3¾ cups) jellied chicken stock (bouillon)
1 teaspoon salt
½ teaspoon freshly ground black pepper
¼ pint (⅔ cup) double (heavy) cream
2 tablespoons (3T) chopped chives

Melt the butter and cook the leeks, onion and celery for 3 minutes. Do not allow the vegetables to brown. Add the potatoes and pour in the stock. Bring to the boil and add the seasonings. Simmer gently for 20-30 minutes until the potatoes are soft.

Allow to cool slightly then pour the soup into the goblet of the blender together with the cream. Turn the speed to low, then gradually increase to maximum and blend until smooth.

Chill well before serving, garnished with the chopped chives.

Serves 4

Cream of Celery Soup

1 head of celery, washed, trimmed and roughly chopped
1 onion, chopped
2 oz. (¼ cup) butter
1½ pints (3¾ cups) chicken stock (bouillon)
¼ teaspoon ground mace
bouquet garni
salt
freshly ground black pepper
1 oz. (¼ cup) flour
½ pint (1¼ cups) milk
4-6 tablespoons (⅓-½ cup) single (light) cream
few celery leaves to garnish

Fry the celery and onion in the butter until softened but not browned. Add the stock, mace, bouquet garni and seasoning to taste. Bring to the boil, cover and simmer for 45 minutes.

Remove the bouquet garni and allow the soup to cool slightly. Pour into the blender goblet and emulsify until smooth. Return to the pan. Blend the flour with a little of the milk, then add to the soup, stirring constantly. Add the remaining milk and bring to the boil. Simmer for 5 minutes and adjust the seasoning, if necessary.

Pour the soup into individual bowls and add a spoonful of cream to each serving. Garnish with celery leaves.

Serves 4-6

Kidney Soup

½ lb. ox kidney, skinned, cored and chopped
1 oz. (¼ cup) flour
2 onions, chopped
1½ oz. (3T) butter
2 pints (5 cups) beef stock (bouillon)
salt and pepper
bouquet garni
½ teaspoon lemon juice
1-2 tablespoons chopped fresh parsley

Toss the chopped kidney in the flour. Sauté the kidney and onions in the butter for 3-4 minutes until lightly browned. Stir in the stock, salt, pepper, bouquet garni and lemon juice. Bring to the boil, cover and simmer for 1½ hours. Cool slightly and skim the soup, if necessary. Remove the bouquet garni. Pour into the blender goblet and emulsify until smooth. Return to the pan and reheat. Check the seasoning.

Pour the soup into a warmed tureen or individual soup bowls. Sprinkle with chopped parsley and serve with crusty French bread.

Serves 4-6

Gazpacho

1 ¼ lb. ripe tomatoes, skinned and quartered
1 onion, chopped
½ green pepper, cored, seeded and chopped
½ red pepper, cored, seeded and chopped
½ cucumber, peeled and chopped
1 clove garlic, crushed
6 tablespoons (½ cup) oil
3 tablespoons (¼ cup) lemon juice
¼ pint (⅔ cup) chicken stock (bouillon)
8 oz. (1 cup) tomato juice
1 teaspoon celery salt
½ teaspoon black pepper
few drops of Tabasco sauce
sprig of fresh mint to garnish

Discard the tomato seeds. Place the pulp, together with the remaining ingredients in the blender goblet. Turn the speed to maximum and reduce to a purée.

Pour into individual bowls or a tureen and chill well. Garnish with the mint before serving, accompanied by small bowls of croûtons, chopped cucumber, onion, tomatoes, peppers and olives.

Serves 4-6

Russian Puffs

16 small choux puffs, see page 11

Filling:

1 clove garlic, crushed
8 oz. (2 cups) cream cheese
2 tablespoons (3T) single (light) cream
salt
freshly ground black pepper
1 teaspoon lemon juice
1 teaspoon lemon rind
2 tablespoons (3T) smoked cod roe

Garnish:

lemon slices
capers

Make the choux puffs and allow to cool completely.

Place all the filling ingredients in the blender goblet. Turn the speed to slow, then gradually increase the speed as the mixture becomes smooth and evenly blended.

Spoon into a piping bag fitted with a small fluted nozzle. Insert the nozzle into the slits in the puffs and pipe in the filling. Pile onto a serving plate. Garnish with lemon slices and capers.

Makes 16 puffs

GAZPACHO *(Photograph: Olives from Spain)*

Devilled Eggs

3 eggs, hard-boiled and shelled
3 sticks celery, washed
6 oz. (¾ cup) cream cheese, softened
few drops of anchovy essence
½ teaspoon salt
½ teaspoon black pepper

Garnish:
stuffed green olives, sliced

Sauce:
3 tablespoons (¼ cup) Worcestershire sauce
2 tablespoons (3T) tomato ketchup (catsup)
1 lemon, juice and grated rind
few drops of Tabasco sauce
1 tablespoon tomato chutney
1 teaspoon made mustard
½ teaspoon freshly ground black pepper

Cut the eggs in half lengthwise and carefully remove the yolks with a teaspoon. Cut the celery into 3 inch pieces. Arrange the egg whites and celery on a serving dish.

Put the yolks, cream cheese, anchovy essence, salt and pepper in the blender goblet. Turn the speed to minimum, then increase to maximum and blend until smooth.

Spoon the mixture into a piping bag fitted with a fluted nozzle and pipe into the egg whites and celery. Garnish with the olives.

Just before serving, place all the sauce ingredients in the blender goblet. Turn the speed to maximum to blend well. Pour a little over each egg. Serve the remainder separately.

Serves 3

Savoury Cheese Mousse

½ oz. (1T) gelatine
4 tablespoons (⅓ cup) water
4 oz. Danish blue cheese
¼ pint (⅔ cup) double (heavy) cream
½ teaspoon thyme
½ teaspoon sage
2 oz. (½ cup) shelled walnuts, halved
2 eggs, separated
2 tablespoons tomato ketchup (catsup)

Garnish:
4 oz. (1 cup) black grapes
1 oz. (¼ cup) walnut halves
few lettuce leaves

Dissolve the gelatine in the water in a small bowl over a saucepan of hot water. Crumble the cheese.

Pour the cream into the mixer bowl and beat on a low speed until it stands in soft peaks. Beat in the cheese and herbs.

Place the nuts in the blender goblet and chop roughly. With clean, dry beaters and a clean bowl, whisk the egg whites until stiff.

Cream together the egg yolks and tomato ketchup, then fold into the cream, together with the gelatine and nuts. Gently fold in the egg whites and pour into a ring mould. Leave to set in a cool place.

Unmould onto an attractive serving plate and pile black grapes and nuts into the centre. Arrange lettuce leaves around the base.

Serves 4-6

Cheese Puffs

4 oz. (1 cup) plain (all-purpose) flour
½ teaspoon dry mustard
½ teaspoon garlic salt
1 egg, separated
8 fl. oz. (1 cup) beer
1 tablespoon oil
1 lb. cheese, preferably Gruyère
oil for deep frying

Sift 2 oz. (½ cup) flour, mustard and garlic salt into the mixer bowl. Make a well in the centre and add the egg yolk. With the speed on maximum, beat, gradually adding the beer and oil to form a smooth batter. Cover the bowl and leave for 1 hour.

With clean beaters, whisk the egg white on maximum speed until it stands in stiff peaks. Fold into the batter.

Cut the cheese into small cubes. Heat the oil to a temperature of 375°F. Roll the cheese cubes in the remaining flour then dip into the batter. Deep fry in the oil until golden brown. Drain and serve either hot or cold.

Makes about 40 puffs

Avocado and Chicken Mould

½ oz. (1T) gelatine
3 tablespoons (¼ cup) water
½ pint (1¼ cups) apple juice
½ teaspoon onion salt
2 ripe avocados
1 tablespoon lemon juice
4 oz. (½ cup) chicken pâté
4 tablespoons (⅓ cup) mayonnaise
½ teaspoon black pepper
Garnish:
4 oz. (½ cup) full fat soft cream cheese
lemon slices, halved
few lettuce leaves

Place the gelatine and water in a bowl over a pan of hot water. Stir until the gelatine has dissolved. Remove from the heat and stir in the apple juice and onion salt.

Peel the avocados. Place the flesh, lemon juice, chicken pâté, mayonnaise and black pepper in the blender goblet. Turn the speed to slow and gradually increase to medium until the mixture is smooth. Slowly pour in the gelatine and apple juice and continue to blend until thoroughly incorporated.

Pour into a lightly greased 1½ pint (3¾ cup) mould or 6 individual ones. Place in the refrigerator and leave until set.

Just before serving, unmould onto a plate and decorate with rosettes of whipped cream cheese, lemon slices and lettuce leaves.
Serves 6

Sweetcorn Salad

1 lb. sweetcorn, cooked
4 oz. (1 cup) onion, diced
2 tablespoons (3T) mayonnaise
2 tablespoons (3T) single (light) cream
1 tablespoon lemon juice
1½ tablespoons (2T) apricot jam, strained
1 teaspoon salt
¼ teaspoon black pepper
2 teaspoons paprika
¼ teaspoon cayenne pepper
1 tablespoon mild curry powder
1 clove garlic, crushed
chopped chives to garnish

Mix the sweetcorn and onion together in a large bowl.

Beat the remaining ingredients, except the chives, together in the blender. Pour over the vegetables and toss well so they are evenly coated. Turn into the serving dish and chill for 30 minutes.

Garnish with the chopped chives before serving.
Serves 4-6

AVOCADO AND CHICKEN MOULD *(Photograph: Mattessons)*

Guacamole Ring

3 large ripe avocados, halved and stoned
3 tablespoons (¼ cup) mayonnaise
juice of 1 lemon
2 tablespoons (3T) tomato purée
¼ teaspoon cayenne pepper
½ teaspoon salt
¼ teaspoon black pepper
1 tablespoon French mustard
2 teaspoons Worcestershire sauce
½ pint (1¼ cups) double (heavy) cream
1 oz. (2T) gelatine
4 tablespoons (⅓ cup) warm water
Garnish:
1 tomato, sliced
1 green pepper, sliced

Place the avocado flesh, mayonnaise, lemon juice, tomato purée and seasonings in the blender goblet. Beginning with the speed on minimum, then increasing to maximum, blend the ingredients together to form a smooth mixture.

Pour the cream into the mixer bowl. With the speed on minimum, beat until it stands in soft peaks. Gradually fold the avocado mixture into the cream.

Place the gelatine and water in a bowl over a pan of hot water. Stir until dissolved then fold into the avocado mixture. Pour into a greased 9 inch ring mould and leave for at least 4 hours to set.

Turn onto a serving plate. Garnish with the sliced tomato and pepper and serve immediately.

Serves 6-8

Quick Liver Terrine

12 oz. liver sausage
2 tablespoons (3T) double (heavy) cream
3 tablespoons (¼ cup) mayonnaise
1 tablespoon chopped onion
1½ teaspoons dried mixed herbs
1 teaspoon salt
½ teaspoon freshly ground black pepper
1 tablespoon lemon juice

Place all the ingredients in the goblet of the blender. Turn the speed to slow, gradually increasing to medium as the mixture begins to combine.

Turn into a terrine or suitable serving dish and chill for at least 30 minutes. Serve with crispbreads.

Serves 4-6

Spanish Chicken Croquettes

½ pint (1 ¼ cups) white sauce (binding consistency), see page 34
½ teaspoon dried thyme
½ teaspoon dried marjoram
½ teaspoon dry mustard
½ teaspoon paprika
1 tablespoon chopped capers
1 lemon, juice and grated rind
8 oz. cooked chicken, finely diced
3-4 oz. water biscuits (crackers)
oil for deep frying
1 egg, beaten

Prepare the white sauce, adding the herbs, seasoning, capers, lemon rind and juice before blending. Add the chicken to the cooked sauce. Leave in a cool place to become quite cold.

Break the biscuits into pieces. Turn the blender to a high speed and drop in a few biscuit pieces at a time to form fairly small crumbs. Turn out onto a plate.

Heat the oil in a deep fat frying pan. Form the chicken mixture into 12 small balls. Dip in the beaten egg, then coat with the biscuit crumbs. Lower the croquettes, a few at a time, into the hot oil and cook until golden brown. Drain on kitchen paper.

Serve hot or cold.

Makes 12

Kipper Pâté

8 oz. kipper fillets, flaked
¼ pint (⅔ cup) soured cream
5 oz. (1 cup + 1T) cottage cheese, sieved
1 small lemon, juice and grated rind
1 teaspoon mustard
1 teaspoon salt
½ teaspoon freshly ground black pepper
1 teaspoon dried mixed herbs

Garnish:
parsley sprigs
lemon slices

Place all the ingredients in the goblet of the blender. Turn to a slow speed and as the mixture begins to combine increase the speed to medium. Continue to blend until smooth. Turn into a serving dish and chill.

Garnish with the parsley and lemon. Serve with hot, buttered toast.

Serves 4

Liver and Olive Ramekins

5 oz. (½ cup + *2T) butter*
1 medium onion, chopped
1 clove garlic, crushed
½ lb. chicken livers
1 tablespoon chopped mixed herbs
salt and black pepper
1 tablespoon brandy
1 teaspoon grated lemon rind
Garnish:
stuffed green olives, sliced

Melt 1 oz. (2T) butter and gently fry the onion and garlic until soft and translucent but not browned. Add the chicken livers and continue to cook gently for 2-3 minutes.

Turn into the blender goblet together with the herbs, seasoning and brandy. Melt the remaining butter and pour 2 oz. (¼ cup) into the blender. Turn the speed to minimum, then gradually increase to medium and blend until smooth.

Spoon the pâté into four individual dishes and leave in a refrigerator to set. Pour a little of the remaining melted butter over the top of each dish and again leave to set. Garnish with sliced stuffed olives before serving with toast.

Serves 4

Smoked Haddock Mousse

8 oz. smoked haddock, cooked and flaked
¼ pint (⅔ cup) chicken stock (bouillon)
½ oz. (1T) gelatine
1 ½ tablespoons (2T) lemon juice
3 oz. (6T) butter, melted
3 oz. Gouda cheese, cubed
½ teaspoon freshly ground black pepper
1 tablespoon chopped fresh parsley
Garnish:
cucumber slices
lemon wedges
cress

Remove the skin and bones from the fish and place the flesh in the blender goblet.

Place the stock and gelatine in a bowl over a pan of hot water and allow to dissolve. Pour into the goblet with the remaining ingredients. Blend on a low speed then gradually increase the speed until the mixture is smooth. Pour into a mould or dish and leave in a cool place to set.

To serve, dip the dish quickly into hot water, then invert onto a serving plate. Garnish the mousse with cucumber slices, lemon wedges and cress. Serve individual portions on a bed of lettuce with toast.

Serves 6

LIVER AND OLIVE RAMEKINS *(Photograph: Olives from Spain)*

SAUCES AND SPREADS

Mayonnaise

1 whole egg or 2 egg yolks
½ teaspoon made mustard
¼ teaspoon freshly ground black pepper
¼ teaspoon cayenne pepper
½ teaspoon salt
½ teaspoon castor (superfine) sugar
¼ pint (⅔ cup) olive or salad oil
1 tablespoon wine vinegar or lemon juice

Make sure that all the ingredients are at room temperature.

Put all the ingredients except the oil and vinegar in the blender goblet. Turn the speed to low, gradually pour in the oil through the centre cavity. As the mixture thickens, increase the speed and add the oil more quickly.

When all the oil has been added, pour in the vinegar or lemon juice. Blend for a few more seconds.

Makes about ¼ pint (⅔ cup)

Tartare sauce:
Add 1 tablespoon chopped capers, 3 chopped gherkins and 1 tablespoon chopped fresh parsley to the mayonnaise.

Curried egg sauce:
Add ½ teaspoon curry powder with the seasonings. Stir 2 chopped hard-boiled eggs into the finished mayonnaise.

Remoulade sauce:
Add 1 teaspoon each chopped fresh parsley, chives, tarragon, chervil and onion to the mayonnaise. Blend thoroughly.

Tomato Salad Dressing

¾ lb. tomatoes, skinned and roughly chopped
¼ pint (⅔ cup) mayonnaise
¼ pint (⅔ cup) soured cream
1 oz. (¼ cup) chopped onion
1 teaspoon garlic salt
½ teaspoon black pepper
few drops of Tabasco sauce
1 teaspoon lemon juice
Garnish:
1 tablespoon chopped chives

Place the tomatoes in the blender goblet. Turn the speed to maximum and blend until smooth. Add the remaining ingredients and blend on a high speed until thoroughly mixed.

Chill before serving, garnished with chives.

Serves 6

Yogurt and Cream Dressing

¼ pint (⅔ cup) natural (unflavored) yogurt
¼ pint (⅔ cup) single (light) cream
½ teaspoon salt
¼ teaspoon black pepper
4 tablespoons (⅓ cup) lemon juice
2 teaspoons chopped fresh mint

Place all the ingredients in the goblet of the blender. Turn the speed to maximum and blend for 15-20 seconds.

Chill before serving.

Serves 4-6

French Dressing

6 tablespoons (½ cup) olive or salad oil
4 tablespoons (⅓ cup) white wine vinegar or cider vinegar
½ teaspoon dry mustard
½ teaspoon paprika
½ teaspoon castor sugar
½ teaspoon salt
½ teaspoon black pepper
½ teaspoon marjoram

Place all the ingredients in the blender goblet and emulsify for 30 seconds.

Makes about ¼ pint (⅔ cup)

Sweet Cream Cheese Dressing

3 oz. (⅓ cup) cream cheese
¼ pint (⅔ cup) double (heavy) cream
2 tablespoons (3T) redcurrant jelly
1 tablespoon lemon juice

Place the cheese in the mixer bowl and beat on a medium speed until soft. Beat in the remaining ingredients, increasing the speed to maximum to give a light, whipped dressing.
Serves 6

Honey Vinaigrette

1 tablespoon clear honey
5 tablespoons (6T) salad oil
2 tablespoons (3T) white wine vinegar
1 lemon, juice and grated rind
½ teaspoon black pepper
1 teaspoon salt
½ teaspoon mustard
½ teaspoon caraway seeds
2 dessert apples, cored and roughly chopped
2 oz. (½ cup) onion, chopped
2 oz. (½ cup) shelled walnuts, halved

Put all the ingredients in the blender goblet. Turn the speed to maximum and mix until the fruit, onion and nuts are fairly finely chopped and the dressing is evenly blended. Pour into a bottle.
Makes about ½ pint (1¼ cups)

Salad Cream

1 egg
1 egg yolk
2 teaspoons plain (all-purpose) flour
1 teaspoon sugar
1 teaspoon made mustard
½ teaspoon salt
½ teaspoon white pepper
¼ pint (⅔ cup) milk
1 teaspoon butter, softened
2 tablespoons (3T) white vinegar

Place the egg, egg yolk, flour, sugar, mustard, salt and pepper in a heavy saucepan and using a hand mixer, beat on a high speed until smooth.

Place on a low heat, switch to a medium speed and gradually add the milk, then the butter. Raise the heat and cook until thick, continuing to beat on a medium speed. Beat in the vinegar, then remove from the heat and allow to become quite cold before pouring into a jar.
Makes about ½ pint (1¼ cups)

SMOKED HADDOCK MOUSSE *(page 28) (Photograph: Dutch Dairy Bureau)*

White Sauce

Binding consistency:
2 oz. (¼ cup) butter or margarine, softened
2 oz. (½ cup) plain (all-purpose) flour
½ pint (1¼ cups) milk
Coating consistency:
1 oz. (2T) butter or margarine, softened
1 oz. (¼ cup) plain (all-purpose) flour
½ pint (1¼ cups) milk
Pouring consistency:
½ oz. (1T) butter or margarine
½ oz. (2T) plain (all-purpose) flour
½ pint (1¼ cups) milk

Place all the ingredients in the goblet of the blender and mix for 30 seconds.

Pour into a saucepan and bring to the boil, stirring constantly. Boil for 2 minutes, still stirring, until the sauce is thick and smooth.

Makes ½ pint (1¼ cups)

Cheese sauce:
Add 2 oz. (½ cup) grated strong cheese, salt, pepper and a pinch of dry mustard to the cooked sauce. Stir until the cheese has melted.

Parsley sauce:
Stir 1 tablespoon chopped fresh parsley, salt and pepper into the sauce before cooking.

Onion sauce:
Add 1 finely chopped onion and seasoning to the sauce before cooking.

Mustard sauce:
Stir 1 tablespoon German or French mustard and ½ teaspoon salt into the sauce during cooking.

Chocolate sauce:
Add 2 oz. (2 squares) grated plain (semi-sweet) chocolate and 2 oz. (¼ cup) castor (superfine) sugar to the finished sauce. Stir until the sugar is dissolved and the chocolate melted.

Rum sauce:
Stir 2 oz. (¼ cup) sugar, 2 drops vanilla essence and 3 tablespoons (¼ cup) rum into the sauce before cooking.

Almond sauce:
Add 2 oz. (¼ cup) castor (superfine) sugar and 2-3 drops almond essence to the sauce. Stir until the sugar is dissolved.

Tomato Sauce

3 lb. tomatoes, roughly chopped
2 teaspoons salt
2 teaspoons sugar
1 teaspoon dried basil
1 teaspoon black pepper
1 teaspoon grated lemon rind
2 oz. (¼ cup) butter
1 onion, roughly chopped
1 garlic clove, crushed
2 oz. (½ cup) plain (all-purpose) flour

Place the tomatoes in a large saucepan and cook gently for 20 minutes until soft and the skins have come away from the flesh. Remove the tomato skins. Add the salt, sugar, basil, pepper and lemon rind.

Melt the butter and fry the onion and garlic gently for 4-5 minutes. Stir in the flour then turn into the goblet of the blender. Turn the speed to minimum and gradually add the tomato pulp, increasing the speed to medium. Blend until smooth.

Return to the saucepan and bring to the boil, stirring constantly. Boil for 2 minutes until the sauce is thickened and smooth.

Makes 1¼ pints (3 cups)

Hollandaise Sauce

4 tablespoons (⅓ cup) white wine vinegar
2 teaspoons finely chopped onion
½ bay leaf
6 peppercorns
¼ teaspoon salt
¼ teaspoon cayenne pepper
3 egg yolks
4 oz. (½ cup) butter, melted

Place the vinegar, onion, bay leaf and seasonings in a saucepan and bring to the boil. Continue to boil until the liquor has reduced by about half. Strain into the goblet of the blender.

Add the egg yolks to the goblet and turn to maximum speed for 2-3 seconds to mix. Turn the blender to medium speed and gradually pour the butter through the centre cavity. Mix to a smooth, thick coating consistency.

Pour into a bowl and keep warm over a saucepan of warm water until required.

Makes about ⅓ pint (1 cup)

Cream Cheese Dip

6 oz. (¾ cup) cream cheese, softened
4 tablespoons (⅓ cup) double (heavy) cream
1 teaspoon grated dried horseradish
1 teaspoon lemon rind
2-3 stuffed olives to garnish

Place all the ingredients in the blender goblet. Turn the speed to low then gradually increase to maximum until the mixture is evenly blended. Turn into a serving bowl and chill.

Garnish with sliced stuffed olives. Serve with crusty bread and sliced raw vegetables such as tomatoes, courgettes, mushrooms, celery, carrots, peppers and cauliflower.

Serves 4-6

Avocado Dip

3 avocados, peeled, stoned and chopped
3 tablespoons (¼ cup) mayonnaise
¼ teaspoon salt
¼ teaspoon black pepper
¼ teaspoon chilli sauce
2 tablespoons (3T) chopped onion
1 teaspoon French mustard
2 teaspoons lemon juice

Place all the ingredients in the blender goblet. Turn the speed to low, then increase to high and mix until the ingredients are thoroughly incorporated.

Spoon into a bowl, cover and chill for 30 minutes.

Serves 6-8

Aubergine Dip

2 large aubergines (egg plants), cooked and peeled
1 clove garlic, crushed
4 tablespoons (⅓ cup) olive oil
juice of 1 lemon
1 teaspoon salt
4 sprigs fresh parsley
½ teaspoon freshly ground black pepper

Place the aubergine flesh in the goblet of the blender. Starting with the speed on low, then increasing to medium, blend until smooth.

Add the garlic and gradually pour in the oil through the centre cavity. Add 1 tablespoon lemon juice, salt, parsley and pepper. Blend on high speed until thoroughly mixed. Taste and add more lemon juice, if desired.

Turn into a dish and chill for 30 minutes.

Serves 4-6

CREAM CHEESE DIP *(Photograph: Olives from Spain)*

Gran Reserva
austino I
Bilbao Wines, London E. 2.

Piquant Cheese Spread

8 oz. (1 cup) cottage cheese, sieved
¼ pint (⅔ cup) soured cream
2 teaspoons capers
1 gherkin, chopped
1 tablespoon chopped fresh parsley
grated rind of ½ lemon
1 teaspoon chopped onion
¼ teaspoon salt
freshly ground black pepper to taste

Place all the ingredients in the goblet of a blender. Turn to a low speed, then gradually increase to high and blend until the ingredients are thoroughly incorporated and the spread is smooth.

Turn into pots. Use this spread on bread and savoury scones.

Serves 6-8

Chicken and Ham Spread

8 oz. cooked chicken, chopped
8 oz. lean cooked ham, chopped
6 oz. (¾ cup) butter, softened
½ teaspoon salt
¼ teaspoon freshly ground black pepper
1 tablespoon grated fresh horseradish
½ teaspoon grated nutmeg
4 oz. (½ cup) butter, clarified

Turn the speed of the blender to medium and gradually add small quantities of chicken, ham and butter. Add the seasoning, horseradish and nutmeg. Blend to a smooth paste.

Spoon into pots. Pour over the clarified butter to seal. Leave in a cool place until the butter has set.

Makes about 1½ lb.

Provençal Spread

9 oz. can tuna fish, drained
4 tablespoons (⅓ cup) mayonnaise
4 tablespoons (⅓ cup) soured cream
2 hard-boiled eggs, chopped
½ pimento, chopped
2 gherkins, chopped
1 oz. (¼ cup) chopped onion
4 black olives, stoned and chopped
½ teaspoon garlic salt
½ teaspoon paprika

Put the fish, mayonnaise and soured cream into the blender goblet and turn to a slow speed until the mixture is just beginning to combine.

Gradually add the remaining ingredients, increasing the speed to medium. Mix until evenly blended.

Taste and adjust the seasoning if necessary. Spoon into pots and serve chilled.

Serves 4-6

Cumberland Rum Butter

4 oz. (½ cup) butter, softened
4 oz. (⅔ cup) brown sugar
1 teaspoon grated orange rind
1 teaspoon grated lemon rind
½ teaspoon mixed spice
½ teaspoon lemon juice
4 tablespoons (⅓ cup) dark rum

With the mixer speed on maximum, cream the butter and sugar until light and fluffy. Add the flavourings and rum, beating on a high speed until smooth.

Chill before use. Serve with rich fruit pies and puddings, especially Christmas pudding.

Makes about 10 oz. (1¼ cups)

Herb Butter

4 oz. (½ cup) butter, softened
½ teaspoon chopped fresh parsley
½ teaspoon savory
½ teaspoon thyme
½ teaspoon marjoram
1 tablespoon lemon juice

Beat the butter on a medium speed until light. Increase the speed to maximum and beat in the herbs and lemon juice.

Makes about 4 oz. (½ cup)

Apple and Bacon Charlotte

8 oz. streaky (fatty) bacon, derinded
1 teaspoon made mustard
3 large cooking apples, peeled and cored
8 oz. white bread
4 oz. (½ cup) butter
8 oz. (2 cups) cheese, grated
1 teaspoon sage
½ teaspoon paprika
½ teaspoon black pepper
½ teaspoon salt
parsley sprigs to garnish

Cut all but 4 slices of bacon into 1 inch cubes. Place the chopped bacon in a lightly greased ovenproof dish and spread with the mustard.

Roughly chop the apples. Put half in the blender goblet and turn the speed to low. Increase to medium and chop coarsely. Turn out and chop the remaining apple.

Break the bread into small pieces. With the speed on medium, add a few pieces at a time to the blender goblet to make breadcrumbs. Melt the butter in a saucepan, add the breadcrumbs and apple and toss to coat thoroughly. Add 6 oz. (1½ cups) cheese, sage and seasonings.

Turn onto the bacon and spread evenly. Sprinkle with the remaining cheese and lay the 4 bacon slices on top. Bake at 350°F, Gas Mark 4 for 45 minutes until golden brown.

Garnish with the parsley.

Serves 4

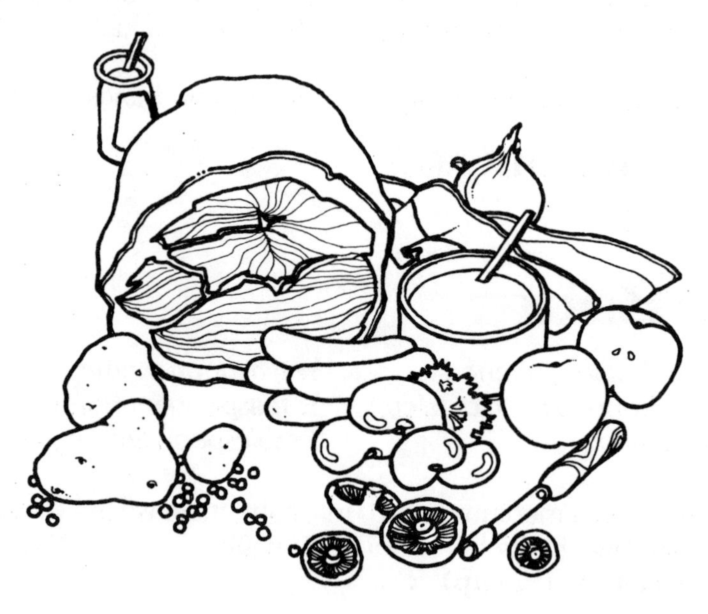

APPLE AND BACON CHARLOTTE *(Photograph: Danish Food Centre)*

Bacon in the Hole

6 oz. (1 ½ cups) plain (all-purpose) flour
1 teaspoon salt
2 eggs
¾ pint (2 cups) milk
1 oz. (2T) lard (shortening)
12 oz. bacon, cooked and coarsely chopped
1 large onion, sliced
½ green pepper, cored, seeded and sliced
2 tomatoes, peeled and chopped
½ tablespoon chopped fresh parsley
½ teaspoon marjoram
½ teaspoon basil
½ teaspoon black pepper

Place the flour, salt and eggs in a bowl. Beat on a high speed, gradually adding the milk, until a smooth batter is obtained.

Put the lard in a baking tin or ovenproof dish and allow to come almost to smoking point in a hot oven, 425°F, Gas Mark 7.

Mix the bacon, vegetables, herbs and pepper together. Arrange in the baking dish and pour over the batter. Bake for 35-45 minutes until risen and cooked in the centre. Serve immediately.

Serves 4-6

Cheese Soufflé

6 oz. (1 ½ cups) cheese, grated
1 oz. (2T) butter
2 oz. (½ cup) onion, finely chopped
1 oz. (¼ cup) plain (all-purpose) flour
½ pint (1 ¼ cups) milk
1 teaspoon salt
½ teaspoon black pepper
½ teaspoon mustard
1 teaspoon mixed herbs
4 eggs, separated

Sprinkle 1 tablespoon grated cheese around the sides and bottom of a 3 pint (7 cup) greased soufflé dish.

Melt the butter in a saucepan and gently fry the onion for 2-3 minutes. Pour into the goblet of the blender and add the flour, milk, seasoning, mustard and herbs. Blend on a high speed for 10 seconds.

Pour into a saucepan and bring to the boil, stirring. Boil for 2 minutes, stirring, until the sauce is thickened and smooth. Remove from the heat and stir in the cheese. Beat in the egg yolks.

With clean beaters and the speed on maximum, whisk the egg whites until stiff. Fold into the cheese sauce with a metal spoon until evenly incorporated. Turn the mixture into the soufflé dish.

Bake in a fairly hot oven, 375°F, Gas Mark 5 for 25-30 minutes until well risen and golden brown. Serve immediately.

Serves 4

Gougère

4 oz. (½ cup) butter
8 fl. oz. (1 cup) water
6 oz. (1½ cups) plain (all-purpose) flour
1 teaspoon salt
4 eggs
4 oz. (1 cup) cheese, preferably Gruyère, grated

Put the butter and water in a saucepan over a moderate heat. When the butter is melted, add the flour and salt at once. Beat on a low speed, increasing gradually to high and cook until the mixture comes cleanly away from the sides of the pan.

Remove from the heat and add the eggs, one at a time, beating well on maximum speed after each addition. Beat in all but 2 tablespoons (3T) cheese. The mixture should be thick, smooth and glossy.

Place heaped tablespoons of the mixture on a greased baking sheet to form a ring. Sprinkle with the remaining cheese and bake in a hot oven, 425°F, Gas Mark 7 for 40-45 minutes until risen and golden brown.

Serve immediately or cool on a wire tray and serve cold.

Serves 4

Sausage and Leek Flan

4 oz. shortcrust pastry (basic pie dough), see page 10
1 lb. leeks, cut into ½ inch pieces
1 oz. (2T) butter
1 oz. (¼ cup) plain (all-purpose) flour
½ teaspoon salt
½ teaspoon black pepper
½ teaspoon German mustard
½ pint (1¼ cups) milk
8 oz. Bratwurst sausage
2 oz. (½ cup) cheese, grated

Roll the pastry out thinly on a floured board. Use to line an 8 inch flan dish. Bake 'blind' at 425°F, Gas Mark 7 for 15 munutes. Remove from the oven and allow to cool.

Cook the leeks in a little boiling salted water for 7 minutes. Drain thoroughly. Cool slightly then arrange the leeks in the flan case.

Place the butter, flour, seasonings and a little milk in the blender goblet. Turn the speed to medium and gradually pour in the remaining milk. Blend until smooth.

Pour into a saucepan, bring to the boil and cook for 2 minutes, stirring constantly. Remove from the heat and allow to cool slightly then pour the sauce into the flan case and spread evenly.

Fry the sausage until lightly browned. Slice and arrange the sausage on top of the flan. Sprinkle with the cheese and bake in a hot oven, 425°F, Gas Mark 7 for 15-20 minutes.

Serve hot or cold.

Serves 4-6

Meat Loaf

1 egg
3 tablespoons (¼ cup) beef stock (bouillon) or red wine
1 small onion, diced
1 teaspoon chopped fresh parsley
1 teaspoon sage
1 tablespoon lemon juice
grated rind of 1 lemon
salt and black pepper
12 oz. (1½ cups) beef, finely minced (ground)
4 oz. (½ cup) pork, finely minced (ground)
2 tomatoes, sliced, to garnish

Place the egg, stock or wine, onion, herbs, lemon juice, rind and seasoning in the blender goblet. Blend together for a few seconds.

Add half the meat and mix on a low speed. Add the remaining meat and blend until thoroughly incorporated. Pack into a greased 1 lb. loaf tin and bake at 325°F, Gas Mark 3 for 1 hour.

Cool, turn the loaf out of the tin and serve cold, garnished with sliced tomatoes.

Serves 4

SAUSAGE AND LEEK FLAN *(Photograph: Mattessons)*

Bratwurst

Savoury Pancakes

Batter:
4 oz. (1 cup) plain (all-purpose) flour
½ teaspoon salt
1 egg
½ pint (1 ¼ cups) milk
oil for shallow frying
Filling:
4 oz. cooked chicken, diced
6 oz. cooked ham, diced
2 oz. Danish blue cheese, crumbled
½ pint (1 ¼ cups) white sauce (coating consistency), see page 34
3 tablespoons (¼ cup) tomato purée
1 tablespoon milk
pinch of sugar

Prepare the batter according to the basic recipe (see page 12). Leave to stand whilst making the filling.

Heat a small amount of oil in a 7 inch frying pan and pour in just enough batter to coat the bottom. Cook for 1-2 minutes until golden brown underneath. Turn over with the aid of a palette knife or toss the pancake. Cook for 1 minute until the underside is golden brown.

As the pancakes are cooked, stack them on a plate with a sheet of greaseproof paper between each one. Continue until all the batter is used.

To make the filling, stir the chicken, ham and cheese into the white sauce. Divide the filling evenly between the pancakes and roll up.

Combine the tomato purée, milk and sugar and spread over the rolls. Bake in a moderate oven, 350°F, Gas Mark 4 for 15-20 minutes. Serve immediately with a mixed salad.
Serves 4

Savoury Scone Ring

6 oz. streaky (fatty) bacon, derinded and chopped
½ onion, finely chopped
10 oz. (2½ cups) self-raising flour
1 teaspoon salt
2 teaspoons dry mustard
½ teaspoon black pepper
1 teaspoon powdered thyme
2 oz. (¼ cup) butter, cut into small pieces
7 oz. cheese
1 large egg, beaten
6 tablespoons (½ cup) milk
6 tablespoons (½ cup) mustard pickle
beaten egg to glaze

Gently fry the bacon for 3-4 minutes. Stir in the onion and continue to fry for a further 3 minutes. Drain on kitchen paper.

Sift the flour, seasonings and thyme into a bowl. Add the butter and mix on minimum speed until the fat is broken up. Increase to maximum and beat until the fat is evenly distributed.

Cut the cheese into small cubes. With the speed on maximum, add the cheese gradually to the blender goblet to grate finely.

Add 5 oz. cheese, egg and milk to the mixer bowl, turn the speed to minimum and mix to form a soft, pliable dough.

Turn onto a floured surface, knead lightly then roll to a rectangle about 9 × 6 inches. Spread with the mustard pickle and sprinkle the bacon mixture on top. Roll up as for a Swiss roll (jelly roll). Damp the edges and press together to seal. Arrange in a ring shape on a greased baking sheet and cut nearly through the ring at 2 inch intervals. Brush with beaten egg.

Bake in a hot oven, 425°F, Gas Mark 7 for 20 minutes. Reduce the temperature to 350°F, Gas Mark 4, cover with foil and continue to bake for 15 minutes. Sprinkle with the remaining cheese and cook for 3-5 minutes until the cheese has melted. Serve warm.

Serves 8

Wholemeal scone ring:

Follow the above recipe but use 3 oz. (¾ cup) plain (all-purpose) flour and 7 oz. (1¾ cups) plain wholemeal (wholewheat) flour instead of self-raising flour. Sift the dry ingredients together with 3 teaspoons baking powder. Serve the scone round warm, split and buttered.

Scones stale quickly so it is advisable to prepare and eat them on the same day.

Spinach Roll

6 oz. spinach
1 teaspoon salt
½ teaspoon freshly ground black pepper
6½ oz. (1½ cups + 2T) Gouda cheese, grated
4 eggs, separated
½ pint (1¼ cups) white sauce (coating consistency), see page 34
2 oz. (½ cup) button mushrooms, sliced
1 oz. (2T) butter

Cook the spinach in a covered saucepan for 10 minutes or until tender. Drain thoroughly.

Place the spinach, seasoning, ½ oz. (2T) cheese and the egg yolks in the blender goblet. Turn the speed to medium and blend until smooth.

Using the mixer, whisk the egg whites on maximum speed until stiff. Fold lightly into the spinach until evenly incorporated. Pour into a greased and lined 11 × 7 inch Swiss (jelly) roll tin. Bake in a moderately hot oven, 375°F, Gas Mark 5 for 10-15 minutes or until firm when gently pressed with the fingertips.

Meanwhile prepare the white sauce and cook for an extra 1-2 minutes to reduce slightly and thicken. Remove from the heat, add the remaining cheese and stir until melted. Sauté the mushrooms gently in butter. Drain on kitchen paper. Add to the sauce and season well.

When the spinach roll is cooked, invert onto a wire tray and peel off the paper. Spread with the sauce, leaving a 1 inch border round the edge. Roll up firmly.

Serve the spinach roll hot or cold with a mixed salad.

Serves 4-6

SPINACH ROLL *(Photograph: Dutch Dairy Bureau)*

Smoked Haddock Roulade

12 oz. smoked haddock
8 fl. oz. (1 cup) milk
2 oz. (¼ cup) butter
2 oz. (½ cup) plain (all-purpose) flour
¾ teaspoon Dijon mustard
¾ teaspoon prepared horseradish
pinch of ground mace
pinch of white pepper
pinch of salt
3 eggs, separated
2 oz. (½ cup) cheese, preferably fresh Parmesan, grated
3 hard-boiled eggs, chopped
1 tablespoon chopped chives

Poach the haddock in the milk for 8-10 minutes or until tender. Drain, reserving 6½ fl. oz. of the milk. Flake the fish and keep warm.

Blend the butter, flour and milk in the blender goblet until smooth. Pour into a saucepan and bring to the boil, stirring continuously. Cook for 2 minutes. Remove from the heat and stir in the seasonings. Using the mixer, beat in the egg yolks, one at a time. Fold in the fish.

With clean, dry beaters, whisk the egg whites until stiff. Lightly fold into the fish mixture.

Spread the mixture in a greased and lined shallow 9 × 14 inch baking tin. Sprinkle with the grated cheese. Bake in a moderate oven, 350°F, Gas Mark 4 for 25 minutes, or until risen and lightly browned.

Meanwhile, in a bowl, combine the hard-boiled eggs with the chives. Sprinkle over the cooked mixture while still hot, leaving a ½ inch border around the edge. Roll up as for a Swiss roll (jelly roll), enclosing the filling. Wrap in foil and allow to stand for 2 hours.

Remove the foil and cut the roulade into 2 inch slices with a dampened sharp knife. Serve with tomatoes and a green salad.

Serves 4

Tuna and Olive Pie

4 oz. shortcrust pastry (basic pie dough), *see page 10*

Filling:

1 oz. (2T) margarine
1 small onion, chopped
7½ oz. can tuna fish
2 oz. (½ cup) cheese, grated
2 tablespoons (3T) tomato ketchup (catsup)
few drops of Tabasco sauce
6 stuffed olives, sliced
½ teaspoon black pepper
¼ teaspoon dried marjoram
1 hard-boiled egg, chopped

Glaze:

1 egg
2 tablespoons (3T) milk

Prepare the shortcrust pastry and leave covered in a cool place.

Melt the margarine and gently fry the onion for 5 minutes until soft but not browned. Stir in the remaining filling ingredients and mix well. Place in the bottom of a shallow 7 inch pie plate.

Roll out the pastry to a circle just larger than the dish. Trim the excess pastry and place a strip around the edge of the dish. Place the pastry lid on top and knock up the edges. Using the fingers and the blunt edge of a knife, form a scalloped edge. With the point of a sharp knife, make a slit in the top of the pie. Arrange 4 pastry leaves on top.

Beat the egg and milk together. Brush the pie with the beaten egg and milk and bake in a moderately hot oven, 400°F, Gas Mark 6 for 25 minutes or until golden brown. Serve hot.

Serves 4

Variation:

Use canned salmon instead of tuna fish. Add 2 tablespoons (3T) finely chopped parsley to the filling ingredients. Use only 1 oz. (¼ cup) grated cheese. Serve the salmon pie hot with broccoli, courgettes or French beans or cold with a crisp salad.

Tomato and Beef Cobbler

1 oz. (2T) butter or margarine
1 large onion, chopped
4 oz. (1 cup) mushrooms, chopped
3 tablespoons (¼ cup) plain (all-purpose) flour
1 beef stock (bouillon) cube
1 lb. minced (ground) beef
15 oz. can tomatoes
1 tablespoon tomato purée
1 teaspoon dried mixed herbs
2 teaspoons English mustard
1 teaspoon black pepper

Topping:
8 oz. (2 cups) self-raising flour
½ teaspoon salt
2 oz. (¼ cup) margarine, roughly chopped
¼ pint (⅔ cup) milk
3 oz. (¾ cup) Cheddar cheese, grated
beaten egg or milk to glaze

Melt the fat and gently fry the onion until it is soft but not browned; about 5 minutes. Add the chopped mushrooms and sauté for 2 minutes. Sprinkle in the flour and mix well. Remove from the heat and crumble in the stock cube.

Stir in the remaining ingredients. Return the pan to the heat and bring to the boil, stirring constantly. Reduce the heat and simmer for 10 minutes.

Meanwhile, prepare the topping. Sift the flour and salt into the mixer bowl and with the speed on low, rub in the margarine until the mixture resembles fine breadcrumbs. Pour in the milk and mix to a soft dough.

Turn onto a floured board and knead lightly. Roll to an oblong 15 × 7 inches and sprinkle with the cheese. Roll up lengthwise and cut into 12 slices.

Pour the beef mixture into an ovenproof dish and arrange the scones overlapping around the edge. Brush with egg or milk to glaze.

Bake in a fairly hot oven, 400°F, Gas Mark 6 for about 30 minutes until the topping is golden. Serve at once.

Serves 4

TOMATO AND BEEF COBBLER *(Photograph: Colmans Mustard)*

Black

Apricot Cream Dessert

5 oz. dried apricots, soaked overnight
3 eggs, separated
3 oz. (6T) castor (superfine) sugar
1 pint (2½ cups) milk
½ oz. (1T) gelatine
¼ pint (⅔ cup) double (heavy) cream
1 lemon, juice and grated rind
Decoration:
whipped cream
glacé (candied) cherries
angelica diamonds

Put the apricots in a pan, cover with fresh cold water and cook over moderate heat until the apricots are tender and nearly all the liquid has been absorbed. Allow to cool, then pour into the blender goblet, turn to a fairly high speed and blend for about 10 seconds until smooth.

Cream the egg yolks with the sugar, then beat in all but 3 tablespoons (¼ cup) milk. Pour into a saucepan and cook over low heat, stirring constantly, until the mixture thickens. Do not allow to boil.

Place the gelatine and 3 tablespoons (¼ cup) milk in a bowl over a pan of hot water. Stir until dissolved. Pour the egg custard back into the blender, turn to high speed and pour in the gelatine through the centre cavity. Leave in a cool place until just beginning to set.

Whisk the egg whites on a high speed until stiff. Whip the cream until it forms soft peaks then fold in the apricot purée, lemon juice and rind.

Fold the egg whites and cream into the setting custard. Spoon into a greased 2 pint (5 cup) mould and leave in a cool place to set.

Turn out onto a serving dish. Decorate with piped cream rosettes, halved cherries and angelica diamonds.

Serves 4-6

Ice Cream

1 vanilla pod (bean), split, or 1 teaspoon vanilla essence
16 fl. oz. (2 cups) double (heavy) cream
3 eggs, separated
2 oz. castor (superfine) sugar
4 tablespoons (⅓ cup) water

Place the vanilla pod in a saucepan and pour in the cream. Heat gently until lukewarm then remove from the heat, cover and leave to infuse for at least 15 minutes. Strain and allow to cool. With the mixer on a high speed beat the egg yolks until thick.

Dissolve the sugar in the water over a low heat then bring to the boil. Continue to boil until the temperature reaches 220°F or when the slightly cooled syrup will form a thread when drawn out between the thumb and forefinger. Allow to cool for 1 minute, then pour onto the egg yolks, beating constantly on a high speed. Continue to whisk until the mixture is thick and frothy.

Whisk the cream on a slow speed until it stands in soft peaks. Whisk the egg whites on a high speed until stiff. With a metal spoon, fold the cream then the egg whites into the sugar and egg yolks.

Turn into an ice tray and place in a deep freeze or the freezer compartment of a refrigerator set at maximum. Freeze for 45 minutes, then turn out and beat well on a high speed. Pour back into the container and freeze.

Makes 1 pint (2½ cups)

Chocolate ice cream:
Melt 4 oz. (4 squares) plain (semi-sweet) chocolate in a bowl over a pan of hot water. Cool slightly then fold into the mixture with the cream. Add 2 tablespoons (3T) rum, if desired.

Coffee ice cream:
Dissolve 4 teaspoons instant coffee in 1 tablespoon hot water. Cool, then add to the mixture with the cream.

Soft fruit ice cream:
Add ¼ pint (⅔ cup) raspberry, strawberry or blackcurrant purée to the ice cream before freezing.

Citrus ice cream:
Add 2 tablespoons (3T) lemon or orange juice and 2 teaspoons grated rind to the mixture with the cream.

Ginger ice cream:
Fold 2 oz. (⅓ cup) chopped crystallized (candied) ginger and 2 teaspoons ginger syrup into the mixture with the cream.

Black Forest Bombe

Chocolate ice cream:
4 oz. (4 squares) plain (semi-sweet) chocolate
6 oz. (1 ¾ cups) cream cheese
4 oz. (½ cup) castor (superfine) sugar
8 fl. oz. (1 cup) milk
¼ pint (⅔ cup) double (heavy) cream
Cherry ice cream:
3 oz. (6T) cream cheese
1 ½ oz. (3T) castor (superfine) sugar
3 tablespoons (¼ cup) milk
3 tablespoons (¼ cup) double (heavy) cream
15 oz. can cherry pie filling
Plain ice cream:
3 oz. (6T) cream cheese
1 ½ oz. (3T) castor (superfine) sugar
3 tablespoons (¼ cup) milk
2 tablespoons (3T) double (heavy) cream

Place a 6 inch loose bottomed cake tin in the freezing compartment to chill.

To make the chocolate ice cream, place the chocolate in a basin over a saucepan of hot water and stir until melted. Beat the cream cheese with the sugar on a medium speed until smooth. Beat in the melted chocolate on a high speed, then gradually add the milk and cream, beating well.

Spoon into ice trays or other suitable containers, cover and leave in the freezing compartment of the refrigerator for about 40 minutes or until half frozen.

For the cherry ice cream, beat the cream cheese and sugar together on a medium speed until smooth. Increase the speed to maximum and beat in the milk and cream. Fold in half the pie filling. Spoon into ice cream containers and freeze until half frozen.

To make the plain ice cream, beat the cream cheese and sugar together on a medium speed until smooth. Increase the speed to maximum and beat in the milk and cream. Spoon into ice cream containers and freeze until half frozen.

To assemble the bombe; spoon the partially frozen chocolate ice cream into the tin and spread evenly around the sides and base. Return to the freezer for about 15 minutes until firm.

Evenly line the mould with the cherry ice cream. Freeze until firm. Finally add a layer of plain ice cream and spoon the remaining cherry pie filling in the centre of the mould. Leave in the freezer for at least 2 hours.

To serve, remove from the freezer about 20-30 minutes before required. Dip the tin quickly into hot water and invert onto a serving dish. Leave in the refrigerator until required.

Serves 8-10

BLACK FOREST BOMBE, ICE CREAM SUNDAE *(page 58)*, BLACKCURRANT MOUSSE *(page 58) (Photograph: Kraft Foods Ltd.)*

Ice Cream Sundae

6 oz. (¾ cup) cream cheese
2½ oz. (¼ cup + 1T) castor (superfine) sugar
½ pint (1¼ cups) milk
juice of 2 oranges
6 digestive biscuits (graham crackers), coarsely chopped
4 oz. strawberries, raspberries or preserved ginger, roughly chopped
1 hazelnut (filbert) or glacé (candied) cherry

With the mixer speed on medium, cream the cheese and sugar together until smooth. Gradually pour in the milk and orange juice, increasing the speed to maximum.

Pour into ice trays or other suitable containers and place in the freezing compartment of the refrigerator or a deep freeze for 1-2 hours.

Remove the ice cream from the freezer and spoon alternate layers of ice cream, biscuits and fruit into 4 sundae glasses, finishing with a layer of ice cream. Top with a hazelnut or glacé cherry. Serve immediately.
Serves 4

Blackcurrant Mousse

1 blackcurrant jelly (1 package blackcurrant flavored gelatin)
4 oz. (1 cup) blackcurrants
2 eggs, separated
2 oz. (¼ cup) castor (superfine) sugar
3 oz. (*¾ cup) cream cheese, softened*
¼ pint (⅔ cup) double (heavy) cream, whipped

Dissolve the jelly in ½ pint (1¼ cups) water. Leave until almost set. Cook the blackcurrants in a little water until soft. Pour into the blender goblet and on a high speed reduce the blackcurrants to a purée.

Whisk the egg yolks and sugar together on a high speed until the mixture is thick, pale and frothy. Fold in the fruit purée.

Cream the cheese with 1 tablespoon of the setting jelly, then fold this together with the remaining jelly into the fruit mixture. Whisk the egg whites until they form stiff peaks and fold into the mixture.

Pour into individual sundae dishes or glasses. Chill until set. Decorate with whipped cream.
Serves 4

Chilled Cheesecake

Base:
12 digestive biscuits (graham crackers), broken
2 oz. (¼ cup) butter
1 oz. (2T) brown sugar
Filling:
12 oz. (1 ½ cups) cottage cheese
¼ pint (⅔ cup) single (light) cream
3 eggs, separated
4 oz. (½ cup) castor (superfine) sugar
¼ pint (⅔ cup) double (heavy) cream
½ oz. (1T) gelatine
4 tablespoons (⅓ cup) water
2 lemons, juice and grated rind
Decoration:
crystallized (candied) lemon slices

To prepare the base, place half the biscuits in the blender goblet. Turn the speed to low to make biscuit crumbs. Turn out and repeat with the remaining biscuits.

Melt the butter over a low heat, remove from the heat, and add the crumbs and sugar. Stir until the crumbs are evenly coated with butter. Spoon into a loose bottomed 8 inch cake tin and press down firmly. Leave in a cool place for at least 15 minutes to harden.

Place half the cottage cheese with half the single (light) cream in the blender goblet and turn the speed to medium. Blend until smooth. Repeat with the remainder.

Beat the egg yolks and sugar on high speed until pale in colour and thick. Whisk the egg whites on a high speed until stiff. Whip the double (heavy) cream on a low speed until it forms soft peaks.

Dissolve the gelatine in the water in a bowl over a pan of hot water. Add the dissolved gelatine and cheese mixture to the egg yolks. Mix well. Fold in the egg whites, whipped cream, lemon juice and rind until just evenly blended. Pour the mixture over the biscuit base and leave in a cool place to set.

Remove from the tin but leave on the base. Decorate with crystallized lemon slices.

Serves 6

Iced Sicilian Dessert

4 eggs, separated
4 oz. (1 cup) icing (confectioners') sugar
½ pint (1 ¼ cups) double (heavy) cream
4 oz. (⅔ cup) raisins
4 oz. (½ cup) glacé (candied) cherries, chopped
2 oz. (¼ cup) glacé (candied) pineapple
1 oz. (1 ½T) angelica, chopped
2 oz. (¼ cup) preserved ginger, chopped

Whisk the egg yolks and sugar together on a high speed until thick and creamy. With clean beaters, whisk the egg whites on a high speed until stiff.

Whip the cream on a slow speed until thickened but not stiff. Fold the egg whites and cream into the sugar and egg yolks. Pour into a 2 pint (5 cup) pudding basin or mould, cover with foil and place in a deep freeze or the freezing compartment of the refrigerator for 1 hour.

Meanwhile, pour boiling water onto the raisins and leave to soak for 10 minutes. Drain well.

Remove the cream mixture from the freezer, turn into a mixing bowl and beat on a high speed for 2-3 minutes. Fold in the raisins, glacé fruits, angelica and ginger. Pour back into the pudding basin and freeze for 4 hours or until firm.

Transfer to the refrigerator for 30 minutes before required to soften slightly. To unmould, dip the basin in a bowl of warm water. Leave for 2-3 seconds. Invert onto a serving plate, give a sharp shake and remove the basin. The pudding should slide out.

Serves 6-8

Zabaglione

4 egg yolks
4 tablespoons (⅓ cup) castor sugar
4 tablespoons (⅓ cup) Marsala
2 teaspoons grated lemon rind

Beat the egg yolks and sugar on a high speed until thickened and pale in colour. Place the bowl over a saucepan of hot water and gradually pour in the Marsala and lemon rind, beating constantly on maximum speed. Continue beating until stiff.

Pour into individual glasses and serve immediately.

Serves 4-6

ICED SICILIAN DESSERT *(Photograph: RHM Foods Ltd.)*

Crème Chamonix

4 egg whites
8 oz. (1 cup) castor (superfine) sugar

Filling:

½ pint (1 ¼ cups) double (heavy) cream
¼ teaspoon vanilla essence
3 tablespoons (¼ cup) sugar
2 tablespoons (3T) brandy
8 oz. can unsweetened chestnut purée

Decoration:

1 oz. (1 square) plain (semi-sweet) chocolate, grated

Beat the egg whites on high speed until stiff. Whisk in 3 tablespoons (¼ cup) sugar then fold in the remainder using a metal spoon.

Line a baking sheet with non-stick silicone paper. Trace 6 circles, 3 inches diameter on the paper. Spread about half of the mixture over the circles to form bases. Spoon the remaining mixture into a piping bag fitted with a large fluted nozzle. Pipe the meringue around the edge of the bases to form nests.

Bake at 275°F, Gas Mark 1 for about 1 hour or until dry and golden. Remove from the oven. Cool on a wire rack.

Whisk the cream on a low speed until almost stiff. Reserve one third of the whipped cream for decoration. Beat the remaining filling ingredients into the cream until the mixture is smooth and thickened. Spoon into a piping bag fitted with a fluted nozzle and pipe into the meringue baskets.

Decorate each with a swirl of whipped cream and top with grated chocolate.

Serves 6

Orange and Almond Flan

8 oz. sweet flan pastry, see page 11
Filling:
2 eggs
4 oz. (½ cup) castor (superfine) sugar
¼ pint (⅔ cup) double (heavy) cream
4 oz. (1 cup) ground almonds
1 large lemon, juice and grated rind
1-2 drops almond essence
Topping:
3 large oranges, peeled and thinly sliced
1 oz. (¼ cup) slivered almonds, toasted
3 tablespoons (¼ cup) apricot jam, warmed and sieved

Make the pastry and use to line a 9 inch flan ring. Bake 'blind' in a hot oven 425°F, Gas Mark 7 for 10-15 minutes.

Prepare the filling by whisking the eggs and sugar together on a high speed until thick and creamy. Add the remaining ingredients and continue to beat until smooth. Pour the almond mixture into the flan case. Bake in a moderate oven, 350°F, Gas Mark 4 for 15-20 minutes until firm to the touch.

Arrange the orange slices neatly on top and scatter the almonds over the flan. Brush with the jam. Serve cold.
Serves 6-8

Summer Orange Whip

½ pint (1¼ cups) natural (unflavored) yogurt
6¼ oz. can frozen concentrated orange juice, thawed
1 tablespoon gelatine
4 tablespoons (⅓ cup) water
2 oranges
2 egg whites
sprigs of fresh mint to garnish

Place the yogurt and orange juice in the blender goblet and emulsify for 10 seconds on medium speed. Dissolve the gelatine in the water in a bowl over a pan of hot water.

Grate the rind from the oranges then peel, removing all the pith. Chop the flesh roughly, discarding any pips. Add the rind and flesh to the yogurt, turn the speed to maximum and gradually pour in the gelatine. Blend until thoroughly mixed. Leave in a cool place until just beginning to set.

Whisk the egg whites on a high speed until stiff. Fold into the orange mixture. Spoon into individual glasses and leave to set. Garnish with the fresh mint and serve chilled.
Serves 4-6

Frangipan Meringue Flans

8 oz. sweet flan pastry, see page 11

Filling:

3 oz. (6T) butter, softened
3 oz. (6T) castor (superfine) sugar
3 egg yolks
4 oz. (1 cup) ground almonds
4 tablespoons (⅓ cup) strawberry jam

Meringue:

3 egg whites
4 oz. (½ cup) castor (superfine) sugar

Decoration:

glacé (candied) cherries
angelica diamonds

Prepare the pastry and use to line 4 individual ovenproof dishes. Bake 'blind' in a fairly hot oven, 425°F, Gas Mark 7 for 10-15 minutes.

Prepare the filling by creaming the butter and sugar together on a medium setting until light and fluffy. Beat in the egg yolks. Reduce the speed to low and add the ground almonds.

When the pastry cases are cooked, remove from the oven. Leave to cool slightly whilst making the meringue. Whisk the egg whites on a high speed until stiff. Beat in half the sugar, then fold in the remainder.

Spread the base of each flan with jam and top with the filling. Spoon the meringue into a piping bag fitted with a large fluted nozzle. Pipe the meringue on top of each flan. Bake at 325°F, Gas Mark 3 for 20-30 minutes until golden brown, reducing the temperature if the meringue browns too quickly.

Allow to cool then decorate with glacé (candied) cherries and angélica diamonds.

Serves 4

Banana Fritters

4 oz. (1 cup) plain (all-purpose) flour
½ teaspoon salt
1 egg
¼ pint (⅔ cup) evaporated milk
4 firm bananas
juice of 1 lemon
oil for deep frying
1 tablespoon brown sugar
½ teaspoon cinnamon

Put the flour, salt, egg and a little of the milk in the blender goblet. Turn the speed to medium and gradually pour in the remaining evaporated milk, increasing the speed. Blend to a smooth batter. Leave for 30 minutes.

Peel the bananas, cut in half lengthwise then crosswise, making four pieces. Sprinkle with the lemon juice. Heat the oil in a deep fryer to 375°F. Dip the bananas in the batter and deep fry in the hot oil for about 4 minutes until golden brown.

Mix together the brown sugar and cinnamon and sprinkle over the bananas. Serve immediately.

Serves 4

FRANGIPAN MERINGUE FLANS *(Photograph: RHM Foods Ltd.)*

Cherry and Almond Cheesecake

Base:
5 oz. (1 ¼ cups) plain (all-purpose) flour
1 oz. (¼ cup) ground almonds
4 oz. (½ cup) butter
2 oz. (¼ cup) castor (superfine) sugar
Filling:
½ oz. (1T) gelatine
3 tablespoons (¼ cup) water
2 egg yolks
2 oz. (¼ cup) castor (superfine) sugar
¼ pint (⅔ cup) double (heavy) cream
5 fl. oz. (⅔ cup) natural (unflavored) yogurt
2 oz. (½ cup) ground almonds
4 tablespoons (⅓ cup) sherry
8 oz. (1 cup) cream cheese
Topping:
15 oz. can black (bing) cherries
2 teaspoons arrowroot
1 tablespoon sherry

Sift the flour into the mixer bowl. Mix flour and ground almonds on a low speed. Rub in the butter, increasing the speed to medium until the mixture resembles fine breadcrumbs. Stir in the sugar and bind using fingertips to form a soft dough. Roll out to an 8 inch circle and place on the base of an 8 inch loose bottomed cake tin. Prick the surface and bake at 300°F, Gas Mark 2 for 40-45 minutes until golden brown. Cool in the tin.

Dissolve gelatine in the water in a basin over a pan of hot water. Warm the mixer bowl. Beat the egg yolks and sugar together on maximum speed until thick and creamy. Gradually beat in the gelatine. Whip the cream until it forms soft peaks and fold into the mixture with the yogurt, ground almonds and sherry. Soften cheese and fold into the mixture. Pour over the cheesecake base and leave to set. Remove from the tin.

Drain the cherries, reserving ¼ pint (⅔ cup) juice. Arrange fruit on top of the cheesecake. Blend arrowroot with reserved cherry juice and sherry and heat until thickened and clear. Cool and spoon over the cherries. Chill cheesecake before serving.
Serves 8-12

Midsummer Meringue

6 egg whites
12 oz. (1 ½ cups) castor (superfine) sugar
1 teaspoon cornflour (cornstarch)
1 teaspoon vanilla essence
½ pint (1 ¼ cups) double (heavy) cream
1 tablespoon orange liqueur
2 tablespoons (3T) clear honey
8 oz. strawberries or raspberries

With the mixer speed on high, whisk the egg whites until stiff. Add 3 tablespoons (¼ cup) sugar and continue to whisk until stiff and glossy. Combine the cornflour with the remaining sugar and vanilla essence. Beat into the egg whites on a high speed.

Line 2 baking sheets with non-stick silicone paper. Trace 2 circles, 8 inches diameter on one sheet. Spread about two-thirds of the mixture over the circles to form 2 meringue layers. Spoon the remaining mixture into a piping bag fitted with a fluted nozzle. Pipe 12 small meringues onto the other baking sheet.

Bake in a cool oven, 275°F, Gas Mark 1 for 45-50 minutes. Transfer to a wire rack to cool. Meanwhile whip the cream on a low speed with the liqueur and honey. Hull and quarter about two thirds of the strawberries.

Place one of the meringue layers on a serving plate and spread with half the cream. Top with a layer of quartered strawberries or whole raspberries, if used.

Place the second layer on top. Cover with the remaining cream. Decorate with the small meringues and whole strawberries or raspberries. Serve immediately.

Serves 6-8

Strawberry Flan

8 oz. shortcrust pastry (basic pie dough), see page 10
8 oz. fresh strawberries, washed and hulled
½ teaspoon gelatine
4 tablespoons (⅓ cup) water
½ pint (1 ¼ cups) blender cream, see page 84

Roll out the pastry and use to line an 8 or 9 inch fluted flan ring. Bake blind in a hot oven, 425°F, Gas Mark 7 for 10-15 minutes. Allow to cool.

Arrange the strawberries in the flan case. Sprinkle the gelatine over the water in a small bowl. Place over a saucepan of hot water and stir until the gelatine has dissolved. Allow to cool slightly until the glaze is beginning to thicken then spoon over the strawberries.

Decorate the flan with piped swirls of blender cream. Serve chilled.

Serves 4-6

Steamed Jam Pudding

4 oz. (1 cup) self-raising flour
2 oz. (¼ cup) suet
2 oz. (¼ cup) castor (superfine) sugar
1 egg, beaten
2 tablespoons (3T) milk
6 tablespoons (½ cup) apricot jam, sieved

Combine the dry ingredients in a bowl and make a well in the centre. Pour in the egg and milk and mix on a slow speed until evenly blended.

Put half the jam in the base of a 1 pint (2½ cup) pudding basin (ovenproof bowl) and spoon the suet mixture on top. Cover with greased foil or greaseproof paper and steam for 1½ hours.

Invert onto a serving dish and pour the remaining jam over the top.

Serves 4

Mandarin Upside Down Pudding

1 tablespoon golden (maple) syrup
11 oz. can mandarin oranges
4 oz. (½ cup) margarine, softened
4 oz. (½ cup) castor (superfine) sugar
2 eggs, lightly beaten
2 drops of vanilla essence
grated rind of 1 orange
4 oz. (1 cup) self-raising flour
pinch of salt

Sauce:
½ oz. (1½ T) cornflour (cornstarch)
½ oz. (1T) castor (superfine) sugar
¼ teaspoon cinnamon
1 tablespoon golden (maple) syrup
1 teaspoon lemon juice

Grease an 8 inch deep cake tin lightly and spread the base with syrup. Drain the mandarins, reserving the juice. Arrange the drained fruit over the syrup.

Place the margarine and sugar in the mixer bowl and beat until the mixture is light and fluffy. Add the eggs and vanilla essence a little at a time, beating thoroughly after each addition. Fold in the grated orange rind, flour and salt.

Carefully spoon the sponge mixture over the fruit. Bake at 350°F, Gas Mark 4 for 40 minutes.

Meanwhile prepare the sauce. Make the reserved mandarin juice up to ½ pint (1¼ cups) with water. Pour into the blender goblet with the remaining sauce ingredients. Blend for 15 seconds until smooth. Pour into a saucepan and bring to the boil. Cook for 2-3 minutes, stirring until the sauce has thickened.

When the pudding is cooked, immediately invert onto a warmed serving plate. Serve accompanied by the sauce.

Serves 4-6

STEAMED JAM PUDDING *(Photograph: RHM Foods Ltd.)*

Cherry Pudding

3 eggs
3 oz. (⅓ cup) castor (superfine) sugar
3 oz. (¾ cup) plain (all-purpose) flour
3 oz. (⅓ cup) butter
8 fl. oz. (1 cup) milk
¼ teaspoon salt
12 oz. ripe cherries, stoned
2 tablespoons (3T) castor (superfine) sugar

Whisk the eggs and sugar on a high speed until thick and foamy. Reduce the speed to low and mix in the flour. Melt 2 oz. (¼ cup) butter and add to the mixture with the milk and salt. Mix to a smooth batter.

Pour a layer of the batter, ¼ inch thick, into the base of a large baking tin and cook in a hot oven, 425°F, Gas Mark 7 for 5 minutes or until just beginning to set.

Cover with the cherries and pour over the remaining batter. Dot with the remaining butter and bake for 30 minutes until set. If the top becomes too brown, cover with foil.

Sprinkle with sugar and serve hot or cold.

Serves 4

Fudge Pudding

4 oz. (1 cup) self-raising flour
2 oz. (¼ cup) castor (superfine) sugar
2 tablespoons (3T) cocoa powder
2 oz. (½ cup) blanched almonds, chopped
2 oz. (¼ cup) butter, melted
¼ pint (⅔ cup) milk
¼ teaspoon vanilla essence

Chocolate sauce:
5 oz. (⅔ cup) soft brown sugar
2 tablespoons (3T) cocoa powder
⅓ pint (1 cup) boiling water

Place the dry ingredients in a bowl and stir until well mixed. Form a well in the centre and pour in the butter, milk and vanilla essence. Beat well on a high speed to give a smooth, thick batter. Pour into a greased 1¼ pint (3 cup) shallow dish.

Prepare the sauce by beating all the ingredients together on a high speed. Pour over the batter and bake in a moderate oven, 350°F, Gas Mark 4 for 40-45 minutes.

Serves 4

Fruit Pancakes

Batter:
4 oz. (1 cup) plain (all-purpose) flour
½ teaspoon salt
1 egg
½ pint (1 ¼ cups) milk
oil for shallow frying
juice of 1 lemon
icing (confectioners') sugar for dredging

Prepare the batter according to the basic recipe (see page 12).

Heat a little oil in a 6-7 inch frying pan and pour in just enough batter to thinly coat the base. Cook for 1-2 minutes until golden brown underneath, then turn over using a palette knife or toss the pancake. Cook for a further minute until golden brown. Continue until all the batter is used.

As the pancakes are cooked place on a plate with a sheet of greaseproof paper between each one and keep warm in a cool oven. When all the pancakes are cooked, sprinkle with lemon juice, roll up and serve dredged with icing sugar. Alternatively vary the filling and topping according to the suggestions given below.

Makes about 8 pancakes

Apple and mincemeat pancakes:
Combine 8 oz. (1 cup) apple purée (sauce) and 4 tablespoons (⅓ cup) mincemeat. Fill the pancakes and roll up. Dredge the pancakes with 2 tablespoons (3T) brown sugar mixed with 2 teaspoons cinnamon. Brown under a grill.

Peach and walnut pancakes:
Drain a 15 oz. can peaches, reserving the juice. Put aside a few peaches for decoration, chop the remainder. Combine with 3 oz. (¾ cup) chopped nuts and ½ pint (1 ¼ cups) crème pâtissière (see page 15). Fill the pancakes and roll up. Blend 2 teaspoons cornflour (cornstarch) with a little of the peach juice. Bring the rest to the boil and stir onto the blended cornflour, stirring. Pour back into the pan and bring to the boil, stirring, until thickened. Pour over the pancakes and serve.

Cherry and almond pancakes:
Drain a 15 oz. can cherries, reserving the juice. Blend 4 teaspoons cornflour (cornstarch) with a little of the cherry juice. Bring the remainder to the boil. Pour onto the cornflour mixture, stirring, then return to the pan and cook, stirring until thickened. Add the cherries, 1 oz. (¼ cup) chopped almonds and a few drops almond essence. Fill the pancakes, roll up and dredge with icing (confectioners') sugar.

CAKES AND BISCUITS

Honey Sponge

4 oz. (½ cup) butter or margarine
4 oz. (½ cup) castor (superfine) sugar
2 teaspoons clear honey
2 eggs
½ teaspoon vanilla essence
8 oz. (2 cups) self-raising flour
½ teaspoon baking powder
3 oz. (¾ cup) icing (confectioners') sugar
6 tablespoons (½ cup) milk
3 oz. (¾ cup) walnuts, chopped

Butter icing:
4 oz. (½ cup) butter, softened
6 oz. (1⅓ cup) icing (confectioners') sugar, sifted
1 tablespoon clear honey
1 oz. (¼ cup) nuts, chopped
grated rind of 1 lemon
½ tablespoon lemon juice
Decoration:
whipped cream
few walnuts or almonds

Place the butter or margarine and sugar in the mixer bowl and beat on a high speed until the mixture is light and fluffy. Beat in the honey. Add the eggs and vanilla essence a little at a time, beating thoroughly after each addition.

Sift the flour, baking powder and icing sugar together. Fold half gently into the sponge mixture with half the milk. Fold in the remaining flour and milk. Stir in the nuts.

Turn into two 8 inch lined and greased sandwich tins and bake in a moderate oven, 350°F, Gas Mark 4 for 20-30 minutes or until well risen and golden. Turn onto a wire tray and cool completely.

Make the butter icing (see page 84), beating in the honey, nuts, lemon rind and juice at the final stage. When the cakes are cold, spread the icing over one layer and place the other layer on top.

Decorate with whipped cream and nuts.

Makes one 8 inch sponge

HONEY SPONGE, BANANA TEABREAD *(page 74)*, BROWNIES *(page 74) (Photograph: Gale's Honey)*

Banana Teabread

4 oz. (½ cup) butter or margarine, softened
4 oz. (½ cup) castor (superfine) sugar
2 eggs, beaten
1 tablespoon clear honey
8 oz. (2 cups) self-raising flour
½ teaspoon mixed spice
½ teaspoon salt
3 oz. (¾ cup) walnuts, chopped
4 oz. (¾ cup) sultanas
3 oz. (⅓ cup) glacé (candied) cherries, halved
1 lb. ripe bananas, peeled and roughly chopped
juice of 1 lemon
1 sliced banana to decorate (optional)

Place the butter or margarine in the mixer bowl and beat on a high speed for 1 minute. Add the sugar and continue beating until the mixture is light and fluffy. Add the eggs a little at a time, beating thoroughly after each addition. Beat in the honey. Reduce the speed to minimum and lightly mix in the remaining ingredients until just evenly blended.

Turn into a buttered 9 inch loaf tin and bake in a moderate oven, 350°F, Gas Mark 4 for 1 hour. Reduce the temperature to 325°F, Gas Mark 3 and cook for a further 30 minutes.

Turn onto a wire rack and leave to cool. Decorate with sliced banana, if used. Serve sliced and buttered.

Makes one 9 inch loaf

Brownies

7 oz. (1¾ cups) self-raising flour
pinch of salt
4 oz. (⅔ cup) brown sugar
5 oz. (⅔ cup) butter, melted
6 oz. (½ cup) clear honey
1 tablespoon water
2 eggs, beaten

Topping:

6 tablespoons (½ cup) clear honey
1 oz. (3T) blanched almonds

Sift the flour and salt into a bowl. Stir in the sugar. With the mixer speed on medium, gradually pour in the melted butter, honey, water and eggs. Beat until a smooth batter is obtained.

Pour into a greased and lined 11 × 7 inch baking tin. Bake in a moderate oven, 350°F, Gas Mark 4 for 30-35 minutes until golden brown.

Leave to cool slightly in the tin then invert onto a wire tray and remove the paper. Cut into squares. When cold, spread the brownies with honey and top each with an almond.

Makes about 15 brownies

Butterscotch Cookies

4 oz. (½ cup) butter, melted
6 oz. (1 cup) soft (light) brown sugar
2 eggs
¼ teaspoon salt
3 oz. (¾ cup) self-raising flour
1 oz. (3T) rolled oats
1 oz. (¼ cup) walnuts, chopped

Put all the ingredients in a bowl and mix on medium speed until evenly incorporated. Pour into a greased 8 inch square baking tin. Bake in a moderate oven, 350°F, Gas Mark 4 for 20-25 minutes until the top is just firm.

Remove from the oven and cut into squares. Cool on a wire tray.
Makes about 16 cookies

Chocolate Spice Biscuits

8 oz. (1 cup) butter
4 oz. (½ cup) castor (superfine) sugar
8 oz. (2 cups) self-raising flour
½ teaspoon cinnamon
½ teaspoon mixed spice
2 oz. (½ cup) chocolate powder
1 teaspoon vanilla essence
1 tablespoon double (heavy) cream
vanilla butter icing, see page 84

Warm the bowl and beaters. With the speed on medium, cream the butter and sugar together. Increase the speed to maximum, until the mixture is pale and fluffy.

Sift the flour, spices and chocolate powder together. Add to the creamed mixture. Turn the speed to low and mix until just evenly incorporated. Add the vanilla essence and cream.

Shape heaped teaspoonfuls of the mixture into balls. Place on a greased baking sheet about 2 inches apart and gently flatten with a fork. Bake in a moderate oven, 350°F, Gas Mark 4 for 10-12 minutes. Allow to cool slightly then transfer to a wire tray and allow to cool completely before sandwiching the biscuits together with butter icing.
Makes 12 biscuits

Chocolate Log

Swiss (jelly) roll:
2 eggs
2½ oz. (¼ cup + 1½T) castor (superfine) sugar
2 oz. (½ cup) plain (all-purpose) flour

Filling:
6 tablespoons (½ cup) double (heavy) cream
1½ teaspoons instant coffee powder

Chocolate buttercream:
2 oz. (¼ cup) castor (superfine) sugar
2 tablespoons (3T) water
1 egg yolk, beaten
pinch of cream of tartar
2½ oz. (¼ cup + 1½T) butter, softened
1½ oz. (1½ squares) plain (semi-sweet) chocolate, melted
sifted icing (confectioners') sugar for dusting

To make the Swiss roll, prepare a whisked sponge mixture (see page 14). Lightly spread the mixture evenly in a lined and greased 10 × 8 inch Swiss (jelly) roll tin. Bake in a hot oven, 425°F, Gas Mark 7 for 10 minutes until golden brown and springy to the touch.

Turn onto a sheet of greaseproof paper dusted with sugar. Peel off the lining paper carefully and trim the edges with a sharp knife. Roll up firmly enclosing the greaseproof paper. Cool on a wire rack.

Meanwhile prepare the filling. Whip the cream with the coffee powder on a low speed until it is fairly stiff.

To make the buttercream, place the sugar and water in a heavy based pan and dissolve over low heat. Bring the syrup to the boil, and boil for 2-3 minutes until a temperature of 225°F is reached. Pour the syrup over the egg yolk, whisking all the time. Add the cream of tartar and continue whisking until the mixture is thick and cool. Add the syrup a little at a time to the butter, beating after each addition. Finally beat in the melted chocolate.

When the sponge is cold carefully unroll, remove the greaseproof paper and spread with the filling. Reroll, coat with the chocolate buttercream and mark with a fork to give a log effect. Chill for 1 hour. Dust lightly with icing sugar just before serving.

Serves 8

CHOCOLATE LOG *(Photograph: RHM Foods Ltd.)*

Coffee Mallow Creams

3 oz. (⅓ cup) butter
3 oz. (6T) castor (superfine) sugar
1 egg, separated
1 tablespoon instant coffee powder
2 tablespoons (3T) milk
6 oz. (1½ cups) plain (all-purpose) flour
1 teaspoon salt
1 tablespoon golden (maple) syrup
whipped cream or vanilla butter icing, see page 84
walnut halves

Warm the beaters and cream the butter and sugar together on a high speed. Beat in the egg yolk. Dissolve the coffee powder in the milk and add to the creamed mixture. Reduce the speed to low and add the flour and salt. Mix to a soft dough, adding a little more milk if necessary.

Turn onto a floured board and roll to ½ inch thickness. Cut into rounds with a 1½ inch cutter. Place on a baking sheet, prick with a fork and bake in a moderate oven, 350°F, Gas Mark 4 for 10-15 minutes.

Transfer to a cooling tray and leave to cool completely. Meanwhile, prepare the mallow by whisking the egg white and syrup together on a high speed over a pan of hot water until pale, fluffy and quite thick.

Sandwich the biscuits together with cream or butter icing and top with mallow and a walnut half.

Makes 12 biscuits

American Cookies

11 oz. (2¾ cups) plain (all-purpose) flour
2½ teaspoons baking powder
¼ teaspoon salt
5 oz. (⅔ cup) castor (superfine) sugar
3 oz. (½ cup) brown sugar
1 teaspoon grated lemon rind
1 teaspoon grated orange rind
5 oz. (⅔ cup) butter or margarine, roughly chopped
2 eggs
2 tablespoons (3T) single (light) cream

Place the dry ingredients in the mixer bowl. Mix together on a low speed for a few seconds. Add the grated rind and butter. Continue beating until the mixture resembles fine breadcrumbs.

Beat the eggs with the cream. Add to the mixture and beat on a low speed until the mixture combines and leaves the sides of the bowl clean.

Drop spoonfuls of the mixture onto a greased baking sheet, about 1 inch apart. Bake in a moderate oven, 350°F, Gas Mark 4 for 15-20 minutes until lightly browned. Cool on a wire tray.

Makes about 45 biscuits

Strawberry Shortcake

8 oz. (2 cups) plain (all-purpose) flour
¼ teaspoon salt
3 oz. (6T) castor (superfine) sugar
4 oz. (½ cup) butter, roughly chopped
2 oz. almonds, toasted and finely chopped
1 egg
3 tablespoons (¼ cup) single (light) cream
¼ pint (⅔ cup) double (heavy) cream
1 oz. (¼ cup) icing (confectioners') sugar
8 oz. (1⅔ cups) strawberries, hulled
toasted almonds to decorate

Place the flour, salt, sugar and butter in the mixer bowl and mix on a slow speed. Increase the speed to medium and beat until the mixture resembles fine breadcrumbs. Add the nuts.

Put the egg and single (light) cream into the blender goblet and emulsify for a few seconds. Pour into the mixer bowl and bind the ingredients together.

Divide the mixture between two greased 8 inch sandwich tins. Bake in a fairly hot oven, 425°F, Gas Mark 7 for 15-20 minutes or until lightly browned. Turn out onto wire cooling trays and allow to cool completely.

Pour the double (heavy) cream and the icing sugar into the mixer bowl and whip until the cream thickens. Combine the fruit with two thirds of the cream and use to sandwich the two shortcake layers. Decorate with the remaining cream and nuts.

Serves 4-6

Italian Biscuits

2 oz. (¼ cup) butter
6 oz. (1½ cups) Gorgonzola, grated
8 oz. (2 cups) plain (all-purpose) flour
1 egg
¼ teaspoon salt
¼ teaspoon black pepper
¼ teaspoon paprika
1 tablespoon milk (optional)

Using the mixer, beat the butter on medium speed until softened. Add the cheese and continue to mix until blended. With the setting on low, beat in the flour, egg, salt, pepper and paprika to form a smooth dough. If the mixture is too dry add 1 tablespoon milk. Cover and chill for 30 minutes.

On a lightly floured surface, roll the dough into a rectangle, ¼ inch thick. Trim the edges and cut into 1 inch squares with a sharp knife.

Place on a baking sheet and cook in a hot oven, 425°F, Gas Mark 7 for 12-15 minutes until golden brown. Cool on a wire rack.

Makes about 40 biscuits

Coffee Gâteau

1 × 7 inch Genoese sponge cake, see page 14
Coffee buttercream:
6 oz. (¾ cup) sugar
¼ pint (⅔ cup) water
4 egg yolks
10 oz. (1 ¼ cups) unsalted butter, softened
4 tablespoons (⅓ cup) strong black coffee
Decoration:
4 oz. (1 cup) walnut halves
crystallized (candied) violets

Prepare and bake the Genoese sponge. Leave until completely cold.

To make the buttercream, dissolve the sugar in the water over low heat. Bring to the boil and boil for 2-3 minutes until the syrup reaches a temperature of 225°F. Remove from the heat, pour onto the egg yolks gradually, beating all the time. Continue beating until the mixture is thick and creamy. Beat in the butter, a little at a time then blend in the coffee.

Sandwich the cake together with buttercream and spread a layer of buttercream around the sides. Chop most of the walnuts in the blender goblet on medium speed. Roll the sides of the cake in the chopped nuts to coat evenly. Spread a thin layer of buttercream over the top of the cake. Pipe the remainder around the edge and decorate with the remaining walnut halves and crystallized violets.

Makes one 7 inch gâteau

Spiced Honey Buns

4 oz. (½ cup) butter
3 tablespoons (¼ cup) thick honey
2 eggs, lightly beaten
6 oz. (1 ½ cups) self-raising flour
1 teaspoon ground ginger
1 teaspoon cinnamon
1 teaspoon salt
1 tablespoon grated orange rind
2 oz. (⅓ cup) icing (confectioners') sugar, sifted
1 tablespoon lemon juice

Warm the beaters then beat the butter and honey on a high speed. Beat in the eggs. Reduce the speed to minimum and add the flour, spices, salt and orange rind. Mix until just evenly incorporated.

Turn into individual bun tins lined with paper cases. Bake in a fairly hot oven, 400°F, Gas Mark 6 for 15-20 minutes. Transfer to a wire tray and cool.

Beat the icing sugar with the lemon juice until smooth. Coat the buns with the lemon icing.

Makes about 12 buns

COFFEE GATEAU *(Photograph: RHM Foods Ltd.)*

So White
So Fine
So Light
McDougalls
Flour

Raspberry and Chocolate Cream Gâteau

Sponge:
4 eggs
4 oz. (½ cup) castor (superfine) sugar
3 oz. (¾ cup) plain (all-purpose) flour
1½ oz. (⅓ cup) cocoa powder

Filling:
½ pint (1¼ cups) double (heavy) cream
¼ pint (⅔ cup) single (light) cream
8 oz. raspberries
6 oz. (6 squares) plain (semi-sweet) chocolate

Place the eggs and sugar in the bowl of the mixer and beat on a high speed until thick, light and fluffy. Sift together the flour and cocoa. Gently fold into the egg mixture with a metal spoon.

Turn into a greased and floured 8 inch loose bottomed cake tin and level the top. Bake in a moderate oven, 350°F, Gas Mark 4 for 40-50 minutes until well risen.

Allow to cool for 5 minutes in the tin before turning out onto a wire rack. When completely cold, using a sharp knife, cut into three layers.

Pour the double (heavy) cream into the mixer bowl and beat on a low speed until it forms soft peaks. Increase the speed and gradually beat in the single (light) cream. Use two thirds of the whipped cream to sandwich the layers together, sprinkling each layer with a few raspberries.

Melt the chocolate in a basin over a saucepan of hot water. Spread half over the top of the cake. Leave to set. Spread the remaining chocolate thinly on a sheet of lightly greased aluminium foil and leave to set. When set, cut into 1½ inch squares with the point of a sharp knife. Peel off the foil.

Pipe rosettes of cream on the top of the gâteau and decorate with the remaining raspberries and the chocolate squares.

Serves 8-10

Ginger Cake

8 oz. (2 cups) self-raising flour
½ teaspoon bicarbonate of soda (baking soda)
½ teaspoon mixed spice
½ teaspoon cinnamon
½ teaspoon ground ginger
2 oz. (4T) castor (superfine) sugar
2 eggs
4 oz. (½ cup) margarine
6 oz. (½ cup) golden (maple) syrup
3 oz. (¼ cup) black treacle (molasses)
¼ pint (⅔ cup) milk

Put all the dry ingredients into a bowl and mix together. Form a well in the centre. Add the eggs.

Place the margarine, syrup, black treacle and milk in a saucepan and heat until the fat has melted. Pour onto the eggs and beat on a high speed until a thick batter is obtained.

Pour into a lined 7 inch square cake tin and bake immediately in a moderate oven, 350°F, Gas Mark 4 for 1¼ hours. Turn onto a wire tray and allow to cool for a few minutes before removing the paper.

Makes one 7 inch square cake

Fruit Cake

8 oz. (1 cup) butter
8 oz. (1⅓ cups) soft (light) brown sugar
1 tablespoon black treacle (molasses)
grated rind of 1 orange
5 eggs
10 oz. (2½ cups) plain (all-purpose) flour
½ teaspoon mixed spice
¼ teaspoon grated nutmeg
¼ teaspoon cinnamon
1½ lb. (4 cups) mixed dried fruit
4 oz. (½ cup) glacé (candied) cherries, halved
4 oz. (⅔ cup) mixed (candied) peel
1 oz. (¼ cup) blanched almonds, chopped
2 tablespoons (3T) brandy

Warm the mixer bowl. Cream the butter and sugar together on a medium speed until the mixture is light and fluffy. Add the treacle and orange rind. Beat in the eggs, one at a time, adding 1 tablespoon of flour with each egg.

Sift the flour with the spices. Fold into the mixture with the fruit, peel, nuts and brandy. Spoon the mixture into a greased and lined 9 inch round cake tin. Tie a double thickness of brown paper around the outside of the tin. Bake in the centre of the oven at 300°F, Gas Mark 2 for 3-3¾ hours. Test by inserting a skewer into the centre of the cake. If it comes out clean the cake is cooked. Leave in the tin for 10 minutes before turning out. Cool on a wire rack.

Makes one 9 inch round cake

Blender Cream

4 oz. (½ cup) unsalted butter
¼ pint (⅔ cup) milk
2 teaspoons gelatine

Place all the ingredients in a bowl over a saucepan of hot water and heat gently until the gelatine is dissolved and the butter melted. Pour into the goblet of a blender, turn to high speed and blend for 1 minute. Pour into a container, cover and chill in a refrigerator for 2-3 hours.

Return to the blender goblet and with the speed on high, beat until light and frothy. Use for cake fillings, toppings and for piping.

Makes ½ pint (1¼ cups) cream

Butter Icing

4 oz. (½ cup) butter, softened
6 oz. (1⅓ cups) icing (confectioners') sugar, sieved
1 tablespoon water
Flavouring:
½ teaspoon vanilla essence or
3 teaspoons instant coffee dissolved in 1 tablespoon milk or
2 teaspoons lemon juice and 1 teaspoon grated rind or
2 teaspoons orange juice and 2 teaspoons grated rind

Warm the beaters and the mixer bowl. Place the butter and sugar in the bowl. Turn to a slow speed, then gradually increase to high and beat until light and fluffy. Add the water and flavourings and beat for a further 15 seconds.

Sufficient to fill and coat the top of a 7 inch cake

STRAWBERRY FLAN *(page 67)*, BLENDER CREAM *(Photograph: Dutch Dairy Bureau)*

½PT
8
6
4
OUNCES

White Frosting

2 egg whites
14 oz. (1 ¾ cups) castor (superfine) sugar
½ teaspoon salt
4 tablespoons (⅓ cup) water
2 teaspoons cream of tartar

Place all the ingredients except the cream of tartar in a bowl over a saucepan of hot water. Whisk for 5 minutes on high speed. Remove from the heat and leave to cool for 5 minutes.

Whisk again until the frosting stands in peaks and is shiny. Whisk in the cream of tartar.

Sufficient to coat the top and sides of an 8 inch cake

Fudge Frosting

8 oz. (1 ¾ cups) icing (confectioners') sugar, sifted
2 tablespoons (3T) cocoa powder
3 oz. (½ cup) soft brown (light) sugar
3 oz. (⅓ cup) butter
3 tablespoons (¼ cup) evaporated milk

Sift the icing sugar and cocoa together into a bowl.

Place the remaining ingredients in a saucepan and heat gently until the sugar has dissolved and the butter melted. Bring to the boil then remove from the heat and gradually pour onto the icing sugar, beating continuously on high speed. Continue to beat until the frosting is fluffy.

Use immediately as a filling or topping for cakes. Allow to set before serving.

Sufficient to fill and coat the top of a 7-8 inch cake

Chocolate Frosting

2 oz. (½ cup) plain (semi-sweet) chocolate chips
6 oz. (1 ⅓ cups) icing (confectioners') sugar, sifted
3-4 drops vanilla essence
3 tablespoons (¼ cup) evaporated milk

Place the chocolate in a basin over a saucepan of hot water and heat until melted.

Put the icing sugar in a bowl and form a well in the centre. Pour in the vanilla essence, evaporated milk and melted chocolate. Turn the mixer speed to medium and beat until smooth and creamy.

Use as a filling or topping for cakes and biscuits.

Sufficient to fill or coat the top of an 8 inch cake

Variation:
Omit the vanilla essence. Add 2 teaspoons orange juice and the grated rind of ½ orange with the evaporated milk.

DRINKS

Citrus Cup

1 grapefruit
3 oranges
1 lemon
½ pint (1 ¼ cups) tonic water
castor (superfine) sugar to taste
Garnish:
sprigs of fresh mint

Thinly pare the rind from the grapefruit and place half in the blender goblet. Remove the pith from the grapefruit and add the flesh to the blender. Repeat with the oranges and lemon, adding the rind from 1½ oranges and ½ lemon.

Pour in the tonic water and add sugar to taste. Blend on maximum speed for 30 seconds. Strain and adjust the sweetness if necessary. Serve chilled garnished with mint.
Serves 4

Iced Lemon Drink

2 large or 3 small lemons
1½ pints (3¾ cups) water
2 oz. (¼ cup) sugar
crushed ice

Grate the rind from the lemons and place it in the blender goblet. Remove the pith from the fruit and discard. Chop the flesh and add to the goblet with the water and sugar. Blend on maximum speed for 30 seconds.

Taste and adjust the sweetness, if necessary. Place a little crushed ice in 4 individual glasses and pour over the lemon drink. Serve immediately.
Serves 4-6

Tomato Drink for Slimmers

15 oz. can tomatoes
2 oz. (⅓ cup) Edam cheese, cubed
½ onion, chopped
1 stick celery, diced
½ green pepper, cored, seeded and chopped
1 teaspoon salt
½ teaspoon black pepper

Place all the ingredients in the goblet of the liquidizer and blend together on a high speed until evenly mixed.

Taste and adjust the seasoning if necessary. Add water to dilute if liked. Chill before serving.

Serves 4-6

Iced Tomato Cocktail

½ pint (1 ¼ cups) tomato juice
½ pint (1 ¼ cups) natural (unflavored) yogurt
4 drops Worcestershire sauce
1 teaspoon lemon juice
1 teaspoon celery salt
freshly ground black pepper to taste
sprigs of fresh mint to garnish

Place all the ingredients in the goblet of the blender. Turn to a high speed and blend for a few seconds until evenly mixed.

Pour into 4 individual glasses and chill well. Garnish with mint leaves before serving.

Serves 4

Honey Egg Nog

½ pint (1 ¼ cups) hot milk
2 tablespoons (3T) clear honey
1 egg
2 tablespoons (3T) sweet sherry
¼ teaspoon nutmeg
¼ teaspoon ground cloves

Blend all the ingredients together in the blender goblet for 10 seconds.

Serve immediately.

Serves 2

TOMATO DRINK FOR SLIMMERS *(Photograph: Dutch Dairy Bureau)*

Banana Milk Shake

3 small ripe bananas
1 ½ pints (3 ¾ cups) milk, chilled
4 tablespoons (⅓ cup) vanilla ice cream

Peel the bananas, cut into pieces and place in the blender goblet. Pour in the milk and add the ice cream.

Turn the speed to high and mix for 1 minute or until well blended. Pour into individual glasses and serve with straws.
Serves 4

Hot Mint Milk

½ pint (1 ¼ cups) hot milk
2 tablespoons (3T) chocolate powder
4-6 peppermint creams

Place all the ingredients in the goblet of the blender. Turn the speed to high and blend for 30 seconds.

Pour into a cup and serve hot.
Serves 1

INDEX

INDEX